D0955945

The Book of
Fathers' Wisdom

The Book of Fathers' Wisdom

Guidance, Comfort, and Strength
from Father to Child

Edited by Edward Hoffman, Ph.D.

CITADEL PRESS
Kensington Publishing Corp.
www.kensingtonbooks.com

To my wise father

CITADEL PRESS BOOKS are published by

Kensington Publishing Corp.
850 Third Avenue
New York, NY 10022

Copyright © 1997 Edward Hoffman

All Kensington titles, imprints, and distributed lines are available at special quantity discounts for bulk purchases for sales promotions, premiums, fund-raising, educational, or institutional use. Special book excerpts or customized printings can also be created to fit specific needs. For details, write or phone the office of the Kensington special sales manager: Kensington Publishing Corp., 850 Third Avenue, New York, NY 10022, attn: Special Sales Department, phone 1-800-221-2647.

First printing (revised edition): April 2004

10 9 8 7 6 5 4 3 2 1

Printed in the United States of America

Library of Congress Control Number: 97004955

ISBN 0-8065-2570-3

Contents

CONTENTS

Preface

As a licensed clinical psychologist for the past fifteen years and the author of three biographies, I've long been interested in family life's more uplifting aspects. Despite the undeniable conflicts that exist between parents and children, I'm convinced that this relationship anchors our most basic capacity to love, nurture, and befriend others. Without having had the experience of growing up with an interested adult caretaker, few of us would be able to form meaningful bonds with other people.

To say this, of course, isn't meant to downplay the reality of loveless, "dysfunctional" homes. They are far too common in our wealthy land today. But most of us, I believe, feel gratitude and nostalgia when thinking back to our childhood and teenage years. Especially as we get older and grapple with daily child rearing, we often begin to appreciate more deeply the early guidance of our parents. Certainly this has been true for me.

With the current rediscovery of fatherhood as a key feature of family life, I felt it worthwhile to look specifically at the advice offered by famous fathers throughout history. That is, what words of wisdom did they actually offer their sons and daughters? How did they respond to their own children's problems, uncertainties, and questions about schooling, achievement, work, romance, success, adversity, and faith? And, could such guidance from the past still be relevant in a time when teenagers casually carry cellular phones and preschoolers use computers and color printers to make each other birthday cards?

As my research for this book progressed, I broadened my scope three-fold: to encompass the interesting advice offered by well-known figures like Henry James, Lewis Carroll, and William Faulkner to their nieces and nephews; to present lively anecdotes instead of just private letters; and to feature the paternal guidance given to those who became historically significant like Amadeus Mozart, Leonard Bernstein, Richard Nixon, Jimmy Carter, and Mahatma Gandhi.

Of the various books that I've written to date, this one has probably been the most enjoyable to do. It is difficult to describe adequately my excitement and pleasure in uncovering these gems of fatherly wisdom, selected from literally hundreds of biographies and autobiographies, memoirs, and collected letters. But in completing this fascinating project, I would like to share four key insights that seem most relevant in my adventurous roaming through history:

First, it's probably impossible to predict what grown children will most remember or treasure about their fathers. Many of the heartfelt reminiscences I found were not especially momentous in themselves, yet interestingly epitomized paternal devotion or wisdom for their off-spring—whether such qualities shone through science, art, music, sports, travel, or even humor. In a way, this suggests that every moment between fathers and their children has a wonderful potential for long-lasting meaning.

Second, our words of advice can have real impact. Perhaps it has always seemed to parents that youngsters turn a proverbial deaf ear to their guidance, but after closely examining the lives of so many influential people I'm now sure that something does get through, and we should never underestimate the influence our advice has.

Third, the really important aspects of life—love, livelihood, and health—have remained essentially the same over the centuries. Outer circumstances certainly change, but the human heart doesn't. The sentiments expressed in these wide-ranging letters about personal triumphs and disappointments appear as timeless as this afternoon's phone call home, or to a distant college dorm.

And, finally, I'm more convinced than ever that of all human ties, the bond between fathers and children is potentially among the world's most beautiful. We can't always articulate our inmost feeling in this regard, but I'm delighted that some have been able to do so with such enduring strength. As the nineteenth-century poet Henry Wadsworth Longfellow wrote eloquently to his adult daughter Anne, "It would be in vain for me to try to send you any news. I can only send you my love, and that is anything but news. It is as old as you are."

Or, as plain-talking Harry Truman, in a very different era, wrote to his teenage daughter Margaret, "You mustn't get aggravated when your old dad calls you his baby, because he always will think of you as just that—no matter how old or big you may get."

It's hard to be more clear and loving. In a time when fatherhood is rightfully gaining new attention and interest in our society, I hope that these selections—certainly not intended as definitive or exhaustive—will help prove fathers' love and wisdom are enduring and important.

Acknowledgments

This book would scarcely have been possible without the valuable cooperation of many people. The enthusiasm of my literary agent, Alice Fried Martell, was instrumental in bringing this project to the attention of editor Hillel Black, whose literary judgment, good cheer, and patience have been very much appreciated. For their conceptual contributions, I'm likewise much indebted to Edward Grinnan, Dr. Lawrence Epstein, Aaron Hostyk, Neal Kaunfer, Paul Palnik, Dr. Steve Rosman, and Howard Schwartz. Fanny Chang served as a deft translator of Spanish materials. As a longtime (now retired) high school English teacher, my father offered a variety of helpful suggestions from the outset, as did my mother, also a retired teacher.

On the home front, I wish to thank three individuals for their boundless encouragement. My children, Aaron and Jeremy, by insisting often that I take a break, helped me to stay cheerful and balanced—and to put "fatherly wisdom" into challenging daily practice. My wife, Laurel, more than any other person gave me the emotional support to complete this project and fulfill my own expectations for it.

The Book of
Fathers' Wisdom

James Reston

—

Accept Responsibility

James ("Scotty") Reston was one of America's leading journalists for many decades. He joined the *New York Times* in 1940, later served as its Washington bureau chief, and won the Pulitzer Prize. He exerted a tremendous influence on the way people viewed their world.

Reston's first assignment for the *New York Times* was as a member of its London staff during World War II. He experienced fierce bombing by the Nazis in the Battle of Britain.

Reston, thirty years old at the time, greatly missed his wife and three-year-old son, Richard, who were back home in the United States. Stricken with a fever and increasingly depressed about Hitler's brutal conquests in Europe, he sat down one night in the fall of 1940 and made out his first will. Then he wrote a letter to Richard, to be opened on his twenty-first birthday. Later published in Reston's autobiography, *Deadline*, the letter included these words of guidance:

Many of the things we fight for so hard in life in our ordinary peacetime lives are a sham. The life and death struggles of war like this emphasize this point every day. Bombs at least make you think. They blow up all pretense and leave a man naked before his conscience. All petty wars of life, the scramble for money and power, the endless bickering over material things, are replaced by a simpler ideal of life in which love and family predominate. I don't pass this on as a great discovery. I am merely reporting to you what has happened to this whole nation under fire. All around us here, the people under great stress have found a greater sense of family. They are more thoughtful and considerate and at the same time they are wonderfully hard and tough. They are fighting for something outside and above themselves. That, I suggest to you, is the first ideal.

The second is that above all things a man must accept his responsibility. This war came about in the age of irresponsibility. Our own people in the United States did not accept their responsibilities at the end of the first great war of this century; they ran away when a little boost would have spread the ideals of the American Revolution across the whole world. . . .

I entreat, you, therefore, to accept your responsibilities—first to the dreams of the founders of the United States and the ideals of this country where you were born. . . . Live simply and accept your responsibilities.

Alexander Melville Bell and his son Alexander Graham Bell

——

Acquire Knowledge

Best known as the inventor of the telephone, Alexander Graham Bell was raised in Edinburgh, Scotland. As a child, he was strongly influenced by his father, Alexander Melville Bell, and by his paternal grandfather. An educator and inventor, Alexander Melville Bell specialized in teaching deaf-mutes how to speak. Among his inventions was a symbolic code called visible speech, which showed deaf-mutes how to position their throat, lips, and tongue in order to produce intelligible sounds.

But Grandfather Bell had an even greater impact on the growing boy. A professional speech teacher, he had also acted professionally and written plays. Although frail and widowed in 1862, Grandfather Bell persuaded his son to allow thirteen-year-old Alexander—who had been getting erratic grades and behaving poorly at school—to live

Dick (looking at picture-book). "I WONDER WHAT THE NOAHS DID WITH THEMSELVES ALL DAY LONG IN THE ARK?"

Mabel. "FISHED, I SHOULD THINK."   *Bobbie.* "THEY DIDN'T FISH FOR LONG."

Dick and Mabel. "WHY NOT?"

Bobbie. "WELL, YOU SEE, THERE WERE ONLY TWO WORMS!"

with him for a few months in London. In later years, Alexander Graham Bell would proudly describe that experience as "the turning point of my whole career."

Grandfather Bell had a whole plan to help Alexander. First, he changed the lad's entire wardrobe. One of London's best tailors was summoned, and Alexander soon learned that he could not step out the front door unless dressed like a gentleman, complete with Eton jacket, kid gloves, tall silk hat and cane.

Next, Grandfather Bell went to work on Alexander's language skills and diction. Together they read through several of Shakespeare's plays, and Alexander learned speeches from *Hamlet, Macbeth*, and *Julius Caesar*. Then Grandfather Bell made sure that Alexander put aside light reading and applied himself instead to serious studies. Unlike his son Melville, Grandfather trusted Alexander to handle a regular allowance without constantly having to account for his expenses, and this gave the youth a greater sense of independence and responsibility. As a result, Alexander found himself motivated academically as never before and began to plan a university education.

Soon after turning sixteen in March 1863, Alexander received a birthday present and an encouraging letter from his father back in Scotland:

> God bless you, my dear boy, and may you ever be as happy as
> I have tried to make you during your past life! . . . We miss you

sadly when we assemble by the fireside at the cottage, but we are reconciled to your absence by the fact that you are good to Grandpa and have been a great comfort to him . . . and that you are making good progress in your studies. You will have cause of thankfulness all your life that you had the benefit of such a training as my father has lovingly afforded you.

Melville Bell's prediction was borne out sooner than he expected. When he came to London a few months later to take Alexander home, he found a studious, thoughtful young gentleman of dignity and purpose. "From this time forth," Alexander later wrote, "my intimates were men rather than boys, and I came to be looked upon as older than I really was." The years with Grandfather Bell "converted me from a boy . . . into a man."

James Russell Lowell

———

The Value of a Man

As a poet, editor, and educator at Harvard, James Russell Lowell was an influential literary figure through most of the nineteenth century. He was active in the abolitionist movement, and in later decades served as United States ambassador to England and Spain.

Lowell's personal life was marked by repeated tragedy. Before he had reached the age of forty, he had suffered the deaths of three of his four children and then that of his young wife.

In June 1849, Lowell sent this letter of advice to his fifteen-year-old nephew Charles. Bright and talented, and with the right social connections, the boy was envisioned by several of Lowell's compatriots as a future President of the United States. Unfortunately, Charles Lowell was killed in battle as a Union soldier during the Civil War.

Let me counsel you to make use of all your trips to the country as opportunities for an education which is of great importance, which town-bred boys are commonly lacking in, and which can never be so cheaply acquired as in boyhood. Remember that a man is valuable in our day for what he *knows*, and that his company will always be desired by others in exact proportion to the amount of intelligence and instruction he brings with him. I assure you that one of the earliest pieces of definite knowledge we acquire after we have become men is this—that our company will be desired no longer than we honestly pay our proper share in the general reckoning of mutual entertainment. A man who knows more than another knows *incalculably* more, be sure of that, and a person with eyes in his head cannot look even into a pigsty without learning something that will be useful to him at one time or another. . . .

And remember that Nature abhors the credit system, and that we never get anything in life till we have paid for it. By paying for them, of course, I mean *laboring* for them. Talents are absolutely nothing to a man except he have the faculty of work along with them. . . . Patience and perseverance—these are the sails and the rudder even of genius, without which it is only a wretched hulk upon the waters.

Sidonius of Rome

Avoid Bad Company

A wealthy Roman lord living in fifth-century France (Gaul), Sidonius spent many fruitless years hoping to become ruler of the Roman Empire. Well schooled for his time, and with good family connections, he succeeded in serving as first prefect of Rome, then as patrician, but never achieved his ultimate political goal. Even in a dying enterprise like the Roman Empire, the competition was simply too great.

In the year 469, Sidonius was at the height of his political ambition when he warned his son Apollinaire about the dangers of associating with certain types of people:

> The love of purity which leads you to shun the company of the immodest has my whole approval; I rejoice at it and respect it . . . especially when they violate the public shame by shameless language. [Avoid] a fellow whose talk is at once without end and without point, a buffoon without charm in gaiety, a bully who

does not stand his ground [or one] who is inquisitive without insight, and three-times more the boor for his brazen affectation of fine manners. [Avoid too] a creature of the present hour, with ever a carping word ready for the past and a sneer for the future. When he is after some advantage, no begger so importunate as he; when refused, none so bitter in deprecation. . . . Abstinence is his abomination. . . . The more you avoid even a first introduction to such company, the better you will please me.

Charles Kingsley

———

The Perils of Gambling

The nineteenth-century English rector and author Charles Kingsley is best known today for his novels *Westward Ho!* and *The Water Babies*. He became famous for preaching Christian Socialism, which urged the Church of England to actively support economic and social reforms. For a time, Kingsley served as chaplain to Queen Victoria. Just as contemporary Charles Dickens, Kingsley was destined to lose his sons' companionship in their attraction for distant places.

In 1873, the Reverend Kingsley offered his teenage son, Granville, away at school, this impassioned warning about gambling:

> There is a matter which gave me great uneasiness when you mentioned it. You said you had put some lottery for the Derby and had hedged to make it safe.
>
> Now all this is bad, bad, nothing but bad. Of all the habits, gambling is the one I hate most and have avoided most. Of all habits, it grows most on eager minds. Success and loss alike make

it grow. Of all habits, however much civilized man may give way to it, it is one of the most intrinsically *savage*. Historically, it has been the base excitement of the lowest brutes in human form for ages past. Morally, it is unchivalrous and unchristian.

1. It gains money by the lowest and most unjust means, for it takes money out of your neighbor's pocket without giving him anything in return.

2. It tempts you to use what you fancy your superior knowledge of a horse's merits—or anything else—to your neighbor's harm.

If you know better than your neighbor, you are bound to give him your advice. Instead, you conceal your knowledge to win from his ignorance; hence come all sorts of concealments, dodges, deceits—I say the Devil is the only father of it.

I have held the same view for more than twenty years, and trust in God you will not forget my words in after life. I have seen many a good fellow ruined by finding himself one day short of money, and trying to get a little by playing or betting—and then the Lord have mercy on his simple soul for simple it will not remain for long.

Mind, I am not in the least angry with you. Betting is the way of the world. So are all the seven deadly sins under certain rules and pretty names, but to the Devil they lead if indulged in, in spite of the wise world and its ways.

William Randolph Hearst Sr.

Avoid Gluttony

For more than a half-century, William Randolph Hearst Sr., until his death in 1951, exerted a tremendous influence on American journalism and politics. As a public figure, he was larger than life—first as an ambitious congressman, then as a reclusive yet active businessman, living in the famous castle that rises above the Pacific Ocean at San Simeon. Creator of a media empire, Hearst enjoyed a lifestyle of immense wealth and privilege. But perhaps because he had been born into money, Hearst always wanted his five children to be successful in their own right.

In later years, his son William Randolph Jr. recalled having often received fatherly advice through letters, telegrams, and phone calls. For example, Hearst Sr. once wrote to him with the following advice:

> Success is a frame of mind—a mental power—an immutable conviction—an unalterable determination. Circumstances have

nothing to do with success. When you have made up your mind, success is certain. But, if you only half make up your mind, you will never get anywhere. You have to know you can succeed, and be determined to succeed. You must keep your mind on the objective, not on the obstacle.

William Randolph Jr. also remembered that his brothers were sometimes shocked by their father's blunt advice about achievement. He viewed life as a struggle and felt that flattering or pampering his offspring would only lead to disastrous results.

In 1927, Hearst's oldest son, George, then twenty-three, had begun to put on a lot of weight. His father wrote:

> You are getting dangerously stout. Health is important. . . . You eat heavily and you eat often; then you drink a good deal; and you like beer and fattening drinks of that kind; and that is the reason you are getting stout. People who eat a lot WANT to eat a lot. It is just like any other habit—it is hard to break yourself of it, but it can be done. Furthermore, you do not take any kind of regular exercise. You have everything to live for. Put yourself in condition to live.

After gaining still more weight the following year, George telegrammed his father with the humorous news that "Mom has offered me one hundred dollars for every pound I lose. What is your offer? Surely you won't let Mom outdo you."

But Hearst Sr. was not at all amused. On the same day, he fired back the following telegram:

> If you don't lose weight for your own health and good looks, then you won't lose it for a few dollars. Moreover, I think that Mom is wasting her money because if you lose a few pounds, you will take it right back on again and [the] only solution is for you to keep your weight down by moderate eating and vigorous exercise. I will give you a chance to make a little more money. You may have five percent of net profits of [the] *San Francisco Examiner* under present conditions. . . . You would be very wise to cultivate [a] policy of intelligent economy. Wise people who save money have just as much satisfaction out of savings as jackasses have out of spending it.

James Michael Curley

———

Avoid Profanity and Show Respect

Among the last of the old-time political bosses, James Michael Curley became one of America's most powerful "machine" politicians. He served as congressman, mayor, and Massachusetts governor in an era that extended from the presidency of Theodore Roosevelt to the ascendancy of John F. Kennedy. He was also jailed twice for corruption. Curley was a complex man who took graft shamelessly, yet pioneered the New Deal in Boston, building many hospitals and schools.

The Kingfish of Massachusetts, as Curley was sometimes called, was rather puritanical about proper language. During his first term as Boston's mayor, he invited Babe Ruth—then a member of the Red Sox team—to his home for dinner with the family. Feeling at ease during the meal, Ruth had turned to Curley and casually said of a remark, "That's a lot of bullshit, Mr. Mayor." Immediately, Curley stood up in outrage and threw the ballplayer out of his house.

Curley's son Frank recalled having been struck by his father only once in his life—and that was over his use of a slang endearment. When little, Frank enjoyed sitting at the side entrance of their home, waiting for his father's big car to turn up the driveway. One evening, the car appeared as usual, and as his father stepped out, Frank offered a cheerful, "Hi, Dad!"

Curley slapped the eight-year-old lightly across the face, and the boy tumbled down on the Persian rug. "I am your *father* and don't forget it, boy!" he exclaimed, then stepped over Frank's prostrate form, and proceeded to the library.

About half an hour later, Curley emerged to find young Frank still crying on the floor. His anger abated, Curley explained gently, but without the slightest contrition, that a child had to respect his father: He was to be called Father, just as a general was to be called General. Then Curley thundered, "I will not have a word like *dad* introduced into my house!"

Frank tried to explain. He didn't think that there was anything wrong with the word; he had simply picked it up from some of his classmates at school.

"They're shanty Irish," his father replied curtly and with finality. "If they wish to allow such things in their homes, that's their business."

Earl Carter and his son Jimmy

Avoid Smoking

While growing up in rural Plains, Georgia, during the 1920s and 1930s, Jimmy Carter was extremely close to his father, Earl. In later years, farming neighbors and friends generally recalled Earl as the more nurturing parent—the one most interested in the three children, especially in their studies and recreational activities. Certainly, in Jimmy Carter's autobiography, *Why Not the Best?*, he credited his father with having had the more influential role on his character development.

After leaving the White House, Carter reminisced about a particular aspect of this key relationship in his childhood and youth:

> I have never smoked. I have my father to thank for that. He was a hero to me—strong, fair, hardworking, fun-loving, a good athlete, and my buddy when I was a child. I would follow him with pride and pleasure, not only on exciting hunting and fishing

WISDOM—THE FRUIT OF EXPERIENCE.

Young Hopeful (confidentially). "I SAY, ARE YOU GOING TO TRY ONE OF FATHER'S CIGARS?"

Visitor. "YES. WHY?"

Young Hopeful. "TAKE MY ADVICE. DON'T!"

trips but to the hot cotton and peanut fields in midsummer. Daddy had smoked two or more packs of cigarettes a day since World War I, when Americans first adopted the habit on a large scale. The government had given out free cigarettes to soldiers, and, like a lot of other young men, he started smoking then. On several occasions he had tried, unsuccessfully, to quit. In those days he had no way of knowing that cigarettes would ultimately cause his early death from cancer, but he resented the grip of a habit he could not break.

When I was about twelve years old, he asked me not to smoke until I was twenty-one, and I agreed. I kept my promise, and the day I completed the contract I bought a pack of cigarettes and lit one up. I didn't like it, so I gave the others away.

I didn't know until years later that my reaction was typical. Most young people who don't smoke their first cigarette until their twenties never take up the habit.

Unfortunately, my mother, my two sisters, and my brother all followed my father's example and became heavy smokers. The two who survived have broken the habit, but the others died of cancer.

Sam Johnson and his son Lyndon

―――――

Becoming a Successful Politician

Tall, garrulous, and with strong opinions, Texas state legislator Sam Houston Johnson made an indelible impression on his oldest son, Lyndon. By the age of three, Lyndon was following his father everywhere. At the barbershop, Lyndon insisted on sitting in a chair, having his face covered with lather, and, with the back of a razor, getting a shave like Sam. After the family moved to Johnson City in 1913 and Lyndon saw less of his relatives, "a feverish eagerness to resemble his father took possession of him," according to Lyndon's sister. He looked to him as a "partner, a buddy."

Lyndon later recalled, "I wanted to copy my father always, emulate him, do the things he did. He loved the outdoors and I grew to love the outdoors. He loved political life and public service. I followed him as a child and participated in it." Even as a youngster, he would tell friends that "I want to wind up just like my daddy, gettin' pensions for old people."

Lyndon had an intense interest in Sam's political doings. In 1914, when Lyndon was only six years old, he handed out campaign literature and attended rallies; at home, he watched and listened as people visited Sam to ask for political advice. Sometimes Lyndon was allowed to sit with the men on the front porch or around the fireplace at night while they discussed local and state affairs. If excluded from one of these meetings, Lyndon would hide in the bedroom next to the porch and listen through an open window to what was being said.

In 1918 Sam began taking ten-year-old Lyndon to the state legislature where his son would sit in the gallery for hours watching all the activity on the floor and then wander around the halls trying to understand what was happening. Often Lyndon would come on the House floor and sit next to his father. Though not an official page, he would run errands for Sam and other House members.

The only thing that young Lyndon enjoyed more than his visits to Austin was accompanying Sam on the campaign trail. These trips proved invaluable in preparing Lyndon for his own career as a masterful politician. Decades later, he fondly reminisced:

> We drove in the Model T Ford from farm to farm, up and down the valley, stopping at every door. My father would do most of the talking. He would bring the neighbors up to date on local gossip, talk about the crops and about the bills he'd introduced in the legislature, and always he'd bring along an enormous crust of

homemade bread and a large jar of homemade jam. When we got tired or hungry, we'd stop by the side of the road. He sliced the bread, smeared it with jam, and split the slices with me. I'd never seen him happier. Families all along the way opened up their homes to us. If it was hot outside, we were invited in for big servings of homemade ice cream. If it was cold, we were given hot tea. Christ, sometimes I wished it could go on forever.

William Carlos Williams

―――

Becoming Your Own Person

When he won the Pulitzer Prize for poetry in 1963, William Carlos Williams had also been a practicing pediatrician for more than forty years. Writing in his 1951 autobiography, Williams had observed that medicine "gained me entrance to . . . the secret gardens of the self. . . . I was permitted by my medical badge to follow the poor, defeated body into those gulfs and grottos."

In spirit and technique, Williams has been compared to Walt Whitman, for both poets used free verse to invoke the essential worth of every object and experience. In July 1944, Williams wrote to his eldest son, William Eric, who was serving wartime duty, and revealed his own, deep experience of fatherhood:

> Proud of you, Bill, real proud of you. A father follows the course of his son's life and notes many things of which he has not the privilege to speak. He sees, of course, his own past life unfolding—

with many variations, naturally. Sees moments when he'd like to speak a word of warning or commendation—places where he himself went wrong or made a difficult decision that was profitable later. And all the time he can't say much.

He can't say anything largely because he realizes that in the present case, the case of his son's life, a new and radically different individual is facing life, that the life he faces is different from the life the older man knew when he was young. But mostly he can't speak because—he can't. It would do no good. Likewise he can't praise, much as he'd like to.

John Addington Symonds

━━━

Beginning a Career

John Addington Symonds was a well-known writer in Victorian England. Though dogged by poor health throughout his life, he wrote books on biography, philosophy, literary criticism, and foreign travel for an enthusiastic audience.

Symonds took an intense delight in fatherhood. His three daughters regarded him as a wonderful companion who often showered them with picture-books and composed poems with fancy illustrations for them. When his oldest, Janet, was still very small, Symonds gave her a pony, and the two often rode across Durham Downs together. Dissatisfied with the quality of their schooling, he later helped to educate them at home, emphasizing the creative arts and sports.

In November 1889, Symonds, who was traveling in Switzerland, sent this guidance to his twenty-year-old daughter Margaret ("Madge"), who was struggling to become an art teacher:

Life is larger, deeper, more difficult, more permanently interesting, more evocative [than] all our faculties, than literature or art or science. And so, I shall not be disappointed even if you do not get just what we both desire for you in the way of art-teaching this winter.

Art is very long, and life, they say, is short. But life, as I have found it, is long enough to acquire a considerable command over art.

The first steps are often tedious and disappointing. If you want to draw well and to color well, you must not expect to get far in one winter. This I do not say to discourage you, but to encourage you. Look around now, learn what you really want, be thankful for the singularly felicitous home you have in London. If you see that it would be better to break up these conditions, and to go in for the severer student life, I shall approve. I trust you down to the ground. And anyway, your character is being formed.

Frank Lloyd Wright

———

Be True to Your Ideals

Frank Lloyd Wright was one of America's most influential and imaginative architects. During a career of almost seventy years lasting into the post–World War II era, he created a striking variety of architectural forms. Wright had seven children, several of whom became architects under his tutelage. His second-oldest, John, especially admired his father's accomplishments and wrote an unusual memoir, *My Father Who Is on Earth*. John was just starting his career in booming, 1920s Chicago when his father offered him this provocative advice:

> Where creative effort is involved, there are no trivial circumstances. The most trivial of them may ruin the whole issue. Eternal vigilance is the only condition of creation in architecture.
> You've got to have guts to be an architect! People will come to

you and tell you what they want, and you will have to give them what they need.

If you consider the house first, you will supply the needs of the client. Wants change from day to day, but a house must embody the needs of those who live in it. The architect must be aware of those needs, the client seldom is. An architect must have the courage to turn away a commission even if he is hungry if his work will not represent his highest ideals. No building has the right to be erected unless it is the working out of some idea, the practical demonstration of some principle at work. Think it over, John; to be an architect is no light matter.

Ben Trillin and his son Calvin

Be a Mensch

The contemporary writer Calvin Trillin is a prolific essayist and poet, as well as television commentator. He displays a dry wit when speaking about public affairs. In the literary world, Trillin is perhaps best known for his regular contributions to the *New Yorker* magazine.

The scion of two generations of struggling grocers, Trillin recently wrote an homage entitled *Messages from My Father*. While reminiscing in this book about growing up in Kansas City, he celebrated his immigrant father, Ben Trillin's, hard-working, modest, and ethical life:

> As a child, I understood that frugality was a matter of character. . . . I understood that my father, who in some ways seemed so Midwestern, had a strong sense that proper behavior was modest behavior—the sense that Midwesterners reflect when they respond to an expression of gratitude or admiration by saying something like, "No big deal!" Even the words to live by that I

DEAR CHILD!

Papa (to Friend from Town). "THERE, MY BOY, THAT'S WHAT YOU OUGHT TO DO! GET A GEE, AND COME OUT WITH THE HOUNDS!"

Little Daughter. "OH, PAPA, TAKE CARE YOU DON'T FALL OFF, AS YOU DID THE OTHER DAY!"

have always associated most strongly with him—"You might as well be a mensch"—lack grandiosity.

The German word *mensch*, which means person or human being, can take on in Yiddish the meaning of a *real* human being—a person who always does the right thing in matters large or small, a person who would not only put himself at serious risk for a friend but also leave a borrowed apartment in better shape than he had found it.

My father always meant for me to be a mensch. It has always interested me, though, that he did not say, "You must always be a mensch" or "The honor of this family demands that you be a mensch," but "You might as well be a mensch," as if he had given some consideration of the alternatives.

Gustave Flaubert

———

Be Realistic About Love

One of the leading French novelists in history was Gustave Flaubert. With its vivid, romantic outlook and written with a literary style embracing realism, *Madame Bovary* is undoubtedly his most famous work. Its subject matter, adultery in a Normandy village, generated great controversy in his time. Flaubert was often attacked by critics as licentious and immoral for writing novels on such subjects.

In this letter of July 1867, Flaubert advised his niece Caroline about love and marriage. The two were very close, and a volume of their correspondence was published in 1906. At the age of eighteen, Caroline had become infatuated with her art teacher, and Flaubert offered some pragmatic advice:

> Watch and reflect, sound yourself all over (heart and soul) to
> see if this gentleman can possibly bring you happiness. Human
> life requires something more than a practical turn of mind and

exalted feelings to sustain it; but, on the other hand, if a bourgeois existence makes you dance with boredom, how can you make up your mind to it?

Now, the very idea of my darling niece married to a poor man is so frightful that I cannot dwell on it for a moment. Yes, my dear, I declare I would rather see you married to a grocer with a million than to a great man without a penny. For if the great man's poverty were not enough to drive you out of your senses or mad with grief, his brutality and tyranny would do it.

It will be difficult for you to find a husband superior to you in intelligence and education; if I knew anyone falling into that category and possessing everything else you need, I would go and get him for you like a shot. You are compelled, therefore, to take a good fellow who is not your equal. But could you love a man who would look down on you? Could you be happy with him? That is the whole question.

Sigmund Freud

Attractive Qualities

Sigmund Freud, the most influential psychological thinker of modern times, experienced strained relations with colleagues throughout his life. He was arrogant toward those who disagreed with his tenet that sexuality is the key factor in human personality. In later years, Freud's philosophical writings were marked by an increasingly bitter, cynical view of human nature. But as the father of six children, Freud had a surprisingly warm, gentle side.

In 1908, his oldest child, Mathilde, was twenty-one and suffering from chronic health problems. With somewhat heavy features and a sallow complexion, she began to despair about ever finding a husband. While Mathilde recuperated in the Austrian countryside with family friends, her father offered this guidance:

> I have guessed for a long time that in spite of all your common sense you fret because you think you are not good-looking

enough and therefore might not attract a man. I have watched this with a smile, first of all because you seem quite attractive enough to me, and second because I know that in reality, it is no longer physical beauty which decides the fate of a girl, but the impression of her whole personality. Your mirror will inform you that there is nothing common or repellent in your features, and your memory will confirm that you have managed to inspire respect and sympathy in any circle of human beings. And as a result I have felt perfectly reassured about your future so far as it depends on you, and you have every reason to feel the same. That you are my daughter shouldn't do you any harm, either. I know that finding a respected name and a warm atmosphere in her home was decisive in my choice of a wife, and there are certain to be others who think as I did when I was young.

The more intelligent among young men are sure to know what to look for in a wife—gentleness, cheerfulness, and the talent to make their life easier and more beautiful.

However old-fashioned Sigmund Freud's counsel to Mathilde, it seemed to have had a bracing effect. In less than a year, she married a Viennese businessman named Robert Hollitscher, who was quickly welcomed into the Freud clan.

Robert Frost

Propriety

Robert Frost was among America's greatest modern poets. To paraphrase one of his own lines of verse, "taking the road less traveled" was the choice he made repeatedly in life. To the chagrin of his grandfather, Frost dropped out of first Dartmouth and then Harvard to become a farmer-poet in rural New Hampshire. The hours on the thirty-acre farm near Derry were long, but Robert and his wife, Elinor, led a simple existence raising four children (a fifth died from illness).

Papa Rob, as he was known to the family, spent considerable time with his offspring as they were growing up. Because they lived too far from town, the Frost children attended no school until they were ten years old; rather, Rob and Elinor taught them to read and write. Studying was called "play time," and play school took place at 10:00 A.M. every day. While Rob farmed, the children trailed after him and happily watched him "botanize" as he called it—learning the names of the different flowers. Then, at the dinner table, they discussed the day's adventures.

Born just after her parents' move to New Hampshire, Lesley Frost was typing at the age of three, spelling phonetically. She was already reading at four, composing essays at five, and writing literary criticism at the age of eight. At ten she entered the seventh grade.

Decades later, she fondly recalled that "evening time" for the children meant a short walk after supper with Papa "to see the sun go down, and hear the birds go to sleep and smell the soft mist rising from the meadow along Hyla Brook. After that, we settled down in the front room, for then being read aloud to . . . came as certainly as night followed day."

When Lesley attended Barnard College, her father wrote her frequent letters of advice. Their subject matter was very broad—from how to cope with difficult courses like Latin ("Keep your balance; the grades don't matter," he counseled) to the art of playing tennis skillfully.

In October 1918, when Lesley innocently described an afternoon yachting alone with an older man, this was her father's immediate reply:

> I wasn't there and don't know all that was in the air, but I doubt very much if Mr. Wheeler should have taken you into his boat. In these things, there is no sure ground under our feet. We don't want to think too much about them, lest we grow too sus-

picious and even evil-minded, but also we don't want to have too much to do with them.

The best way I find is to observe a few simple rules laid down by sensible people for keeping out of danger where men and women meet. Be conventional *pretty* nearly always with men and always with these fellows "old enough to be your father." It's a funny world. You don't want to boast that you have scared as reckless a father as I am into chronic sleeplessness.

Groucho Marx

━━━

The Marxian Way

To an adoring public, Groucho was the best known of the madcap
Marx Brothers. Fast-talking, cigar-wielding—with suggestively raised
eyebrows, rimless spectacles, and heavy black mustache—he had a
unique *persona* in vaudeville, movies, and later on television for over
forty years. In his private life as a father of two, Groucho was also
unusual.

His son Arthur fondly recalled, "In most respects, he treated [my
sister] Miriam and me more like close friends than children. He confided in us about his business and matrimonial problems, we had private jokes that nobody else understood, and he liked to take us with
him wherever he went, provided we wouldn't be too much out of our
element.

"He reveled in the disrespect of his children. He'd pounce on an
innocent remark or incident around the house and build it up into a

routine. And, for my money, this was when he was at his funniest. . . . Basically, he [was] more of a humorist and cracker-barrel philosopher than a straight comic, anyway."

Like his father, Arthur disliked the structure of formal education. But instead of turning to stage-acting for more success as a teenager, he found it in tennis, and began to compete in national tournaments over the next few years. Writing in the summer of 1940, Groucho employed his characteristic wit and irony to offer paternal advice:

> For a tennis bum, you're certainly leading a luxurious life, and I only hope you can keep it up. I see by the papers that it rained in St. Louis yesterday, so that gave you time to eat six meals at the hotel instead of the customary five. . . . I've come to the conclusion that it's not so hot being the father of a tennis player. Hundreds of people to whom I wouldn't talk normally rush up to me and immediately begin a long, involved conversation explaining why you won or lost in the last tournament. As you know, I'm deeply interested in your athletic progress, but not to the degree that I want to discuss it twelve hours a day. Now, whenever anyone asks how you're doing . . . I say, "Don't you know? He's quit the game and taken up squash." This baffles them. A lot of people have only heard of squash as a low-grade vegetable.
>
> We received your wire at eight Thursday morning and read that you were in a hotel at Seabright, swollen up with mumps,

and I imagine pretty well disgusted with the whole tennis tour. Well, that's life. As you journey through it, you will encounter all sorts of these nasty little upsets, and you will either learn to adjust yourself to them or gradually go nuts.

I'm pleased to learn that you have a rich dame who wants to put you up while you are recuperating. How does she have her money? Is it in jewels or securities, or just plain gold? Some night, when you are grappling with her in the moonlight, you might find out. Do it discreetly, for God's sake. Don't come out bluntly and say, "How much dough have you got?" That wouldn't be the Marxian way. Use finesse. Well, I will leave the whole thing to you.

Bronson Alcott

Birthdays Are a Time of Renewal

Bronson Alcott was a prominent New England philosopher and social reformer of the mid-nineteenth century. His notable friends included Ralph Waldo Emerson, Margaret Fuller, and Henry David Thoreau. Alcott is also famous as the father of Louisa May Alcott, who wrote *Little Women* and other popular novels. He created the Temple School in Boston, devoted to spiritual development, and also helped found several utopian communes.

Alcott always viewed parenthood as a sacred trust. When his eldest child, Anna, was born in 1831, he immediately wrote in his diary, "'Unto us a child is given.' . . . As agents of the Supreme Parent, may we guide it in the paths of truth, duty, and happiness. May the divine blessing rest upon it. May its mind be the depository of everything pure, beautiful, and good—its heart of all sweet and tender affection."

In 1839, when Alcott was forty, he offered his beloved Anna this encouraging advice on her eighth birthday:

This is your birthday. You have now lived eight years with your father and mother, six years with your loving sister Louisa, and almost four years with your sweet little sister Elizabeth. Your father knows how much you love him. . . . He wants to see his little girl kind and gentle, and sweet-tempered, as fragrant as the flowers in springtime, and as beautiful as they are when the dew glitters on them in the morning sun.

Do you want to know how you can be so beautiful and sweet? It is easy. Only try, with all your resolution, to mind what that silent teacher in your breast says to you: that is all.

A birthday is a good time to begin anew: throwing away the old habits, as you would old clothes, and never putting them on again. Begin, my daughter, today, and when your next birthday shall come, how glad you will be that you made the resolution. Resolution makes all things new. . . .

When you were a few weeks old, you smiled on us. I sometimes see the same look and the same smile on your face, and feel that my daughter is yet good and pure. O keep it there, my daughter, and never lose it.

Mark Twain

Coping with Personal Illness

Mark Twain, the pen name of Missouri-born Samuel Clemens, is one of America's most intriguing literary figures. In late-nineteenth-century novels like *The Adventures of Huckleberry Finn, The Prince and the Pauper*, and *A Connecticut Yankee in King Arthur's Court*, Twain combined homespun humor with biting social criticism.

Widowed for several years, Twain in January 1907 offered this insightful wisdom to his twenty-year-old daughter Jean, who suffered from epilepsy and was emotionally depressed, undergoing fruitless "treatment" in a private New York hospital:

> Bear with the situation as well as you can, and call back the gentle spirit you were born with, and believe that all people mean you well, for it is indeed so. It is your disease that makes you see ill intentions in them—they mean well by you. When you are moved to think otherwise, call back your winning and kindly

earlier nature and drive away the thought. Think the best of people, do not dwell upon their faults, [and] try not to see them. You will be the happier for it.

Jean followed this advice and actively served as her father's secretary after returning home. But the illness finally claimed her during Christmas week of 1909. Grief-stricken, Twain composed Jean's obituary for the press, then vowed to never write for the public again. He kept this promise and died just a few months later.

William Faulkner

Coping with Fear

In 1942 novelist William Faulkner desperately wanted to join the United States military. Proud of his literary achievements like *The Sound and the Fury* and *Light in August*, he was also eager to serve his country. Faulkner flew to Washington to meet with military authorities. He was a licensed pilot, and though admittedly old at age forty-four, he hoped for a position with the air force. After all, his brother Jack had just received a commission in counter-intelligence and would soon be leaving for England. But to Faulkner's dismay, none of the military branches wanted him.

The following year, Faulkner wrote this vivid letter to his nephew and godson James, who was training to become a fighter-pilot:

> Just remember always that flying is fine, and it gets better, but you've got to stay alive to enjoy it. You will have two milestones to pass, to pay back to the government the cost of training you.

The first one is foolhardiness. A lot of pilots don't get past that. Uncle Dean didn't. He managed to blow most of the fabric off his top wing before he found out he had done something you cannot do.

The next milestone is fear. Sometimes they happen at the same moment. This means that you fail to pass the foolhardiness milestone, and it is too late. But if the fear is not a result of foolhardiness, then you are all right. You have learned, and are capable of learning. You must know fear too. That is, you must know how to beat fear. If you cannot feel it, you are a moron, an idiot. The brave man is not he who does not know fear; the brave man is he who says to himself, "I am afraid. I will decide quickly what to do, and then I will do it."

That will come to you. It happens to everyone who flies and who is not a vegetable. It is no more than a sneeze. Accept it when it comes, pass it; tell yourself, "I am afraid. I don't like the way my heart is acting nor how my mouth tastes. But I know what my hands and feet must do, and I know they will do it, because my brain is running things for the next few seconds, and my brain is too busy to worry about what my heart is doing or my mouth tastes like."

I want you to do well. No pilot can tell you how much you don't know. You will have to find it out, from day to day. But you can remember what good pilots have told you, so that when emergencies come, you will merely meet situations which you have already heard about. You will do things without having to think about them, that your instructors have trained you to do. You won't need to worry about that, if you have listened well.

So expect these two milestones. Pass the first one, foolhardiness, and you can take care of the next one. Expect it, too, accept it and pass it, beat it. When it happens, don't forget to write me about it. Fear is an alarming experience, but I never yet knew it to kill anyone. If you are wise enough to recognize the fear, by that time you are safe. The old trained reflexes, the natural good sense, have already done the right thing.

Uncle Jack and your father are too old to do what you can do, and I must stay in civilian clothes to look after things for us when everybody comes back home again. So do well. Don't try to be lucky. Be happy in training, believe in yourself, believe in your ability to listen and watch and learn from instructors.

John Butler Yeats and his son William

―――

Creativity, Imagination, and Artistic Success

Painter John Butler Yeats moved to New York City in the early 1900s after having lived most of his productive life in Ireland. He was a creative thinker who strongly influenced his spiritually inclined son, the Nobel Prize–winning poet and dramatist William Butler Yeats.

Still vigorous at the age of seventy-five in 1914, the elder Yeats sent William, then middle-aged and living in Dublin, this provocative letter about the nature of true art:

> The chief thing to know and never forget is that art is dream-land and that the moment a poet meddles with ethics and the moral uplift or thinking scientifically, he leaves dreamland, loses all his music, and ceases to be a poet. . . .
>
> We all live when at our best, that is when we are most our-selves, in dreamland. A man with his wife or child and loving them, a man in grief and yielding to it, girls and boys dancing

together, children at play—it is all dreams, dreams, dreams. A student over his books, soldiers at the war, friends talking together—it is still dreamland—actual life on a faraway horizon which becomes more and more distant. When the essential sap of life is arrested by anger or hatred, we suddenly are aware of the actual, and music dies out of our hearts and voices—the *anger subtly present* in ethical thoughts—as is also in most kinds of argument; how many poems has it laid low?

The poet is a magician—his vocation to incessantly evoke dreams and do his work so well, because of natural gifts and acquired skill, that his dreams shall have a potency to defeat the actual at every point. Yet here is a curious thing, the poet and we his dupes know that they are only dreams—otherwise we lose them. With our eyes open, using our will and powers of selection, we, together in friendship and brotherly love, create this dreamland.

Pronounce it to be actual life and you summon logic and mechanical sense and reason and all the other powers of prose to find yourself hailed back to the prison house, and dreamland vanishes—a shrieking ghost.

Albert Einstein

———

Cultivate Modesty

In later life, Albert Einstein was very close to his two stepdaughters, Ilse and Margot. In contrast to his youthful days, he became more interested in other children too, and regretted having not spent more time educating youngsters about science.

Einstein particularly enjoyed children's free-spirited directness. "There has always been something about the innocence and freshness of young children that appeals to me and brings me great enjoyment to be with them," he once told an American friend's son.

Once, at a public gathering, Einstein found himself sitting next to a teenager, who failed to recognize the world-renowned theorist at his side. Delightedly, Einstein engaged the boy in conversation, and, after a while, the boy naively asked: "What do you do for a living?"

With typical modesty, Einstein replied, "I study physics."

"What, at your age!" the boy responded incredulously. "I finished that two years ago!"

In relating the anecdote, Einstein remarked how much he admired this quality of naïveté and frankness in children.

Walt Disney

Daughters Are Special

Walt Disney, the cartoonist-businessman whose name became synonymous worldwide with children's entertainment, was very much enamored of his two daughters, Diane and Sharon. During the 1930s and 1940s, the memory of the Lindbergh kidnapping haunted many famous parents, and Disney took elaborate steps to protect his own children. He allowed no photographs of them to be published and never took them to public events where photographers might even be present. The window screens on their lavish Hollywood home were reinforced. Indeed, the girls were so shielded from publicity that they scarcely knew of their father's renown during the early years.

Diane was six years old when a school chum asked her, "Is your father really Walt Disney?" That night, while Walt was quietly reading the newspaper in his favorite chair, little Diane suddenly appeared. With a reproachful tone, she said, "You never told me you were Walt Disney!"

OUR SCHOOL-GIRLS.

Anxious Daughter (to parent playing in the Fathers' match). "DON'T FORGET, FATHER, TO STAND *WELL* IN FRONT OF THE WICKET, BECAUSE IF YOU GET OUT FOR A DUCK *LEG BEFORE* IT WON'T LOOK QUITE SO BAD ON THE SCORE-BOOK!"

THE BOOK OF FATHERS' WISDOM

On Christmas day two years later, Diane awoke to find a beautiful playhouse on the backyard lawn. It looked like a fairy-tale house out of a Disney cartoon, with tiny leaded-glass windows and a mushroom-like chimney. It had running water, a fully equipped kitchen, and even a telephone.

As Diane looked in wonderment, the telephone inside the playhouse suddenly rang. A jolly voice announced himself as Santa Claus and asked how she liked her gift.

"I love it, Santa!" she said.

Later, Diane was naively telling a neighbor boy how Santa Claus had brought the lovely house.

"Santa Claus!" the boy guffawed. "There were men from your dad's studio putting up that house all day." But Diane refused to believe him.

Disney delighted in finding gifts for the girls. Once the studio nurse said to him, "You're depriving Diane and Sharon by making life too easy for them. There will be no challenges for them if you give them everything."

Disney thought for a long moment and replied, "Girls are different."

William James

———

Dealing with Teenage Depression

William James was the founder of American psychology and perhaps this country's most important philosopher as well. A controversial professor at Harvard, he wrote on such unconventional topics as religious experience, mysticism, and the paranormal. For generations, his own brilliant family was plagued by severe depression.

In May 1900, James wrote this consoling letter to his thirteen-year-old daughter Margaret ("Peg"), miserable at a boarding school near London, where her famous uncle, Henry James, was then living:

> Now, my dear little girl, you have come to an age when the inward life develops and when some people (and on the whole those who have most of a destiny) find that all is not a bed of roses. Among other things, there will be waves of terrible sadness, which last sometimes for days; and dissatisfaction with one's self,

and irritation at others, and anger in circumstances, and stony insensibility—which taken together form a melancholy.

Now, painful as it is, this is sent to us for an enlightenment. It always passes off, and we learn about life from it, and we ought to learn a great many good things if we react on it rightly.

Many persons [though] take a sickly delight in hugging it; and some sentimental ones may even be proud of it, as showing a fine sentimental kind of sensibility. Such persons make a regular habit of the luxury of woe. That is the worst possible reaction to it. . . .

If we find ourselves like that, we must make ourselves do something different, go with people, speak cheerfully, set ourselves some hard work, make ourselves sweat; and that is the good way of reacting that makes of us a valuable character.

Sherwood Anderson

―

Deciding on a Career

The twentieth-century American novelist, editor, and poet Sherwood Anderson was acclaimed for his antimaterialism framed in literary language. But in correspondence with family members, the celebrated author of *Winesburg, Ohio* showed a certain bluntness of style. In 1926 his son John was struggling to decide upon a career. Urging caution before making a final choice, Anderson also seemed to be discouraging John from taking a plunge into an artist's life:

> It's a problem, all right. The best thing, I dare say, is first to learn something so well you can always make a living. . . . As for the scientific fields, any of them require a long schooling and intense application. If you are made for it, nothing could be better. In the long run you will have to come to your own conclusion.
>
> The arts, which probably offer a man more satisfaction, are uncertain. It is difficult to make a living.

If I had my life to live over, I presume I would still be a writer, but I am sure I would give my first attention to learning how to do things directly with my hands. Nothing brings quite the satisfaction that doing things brings.

Above all, avoid taking the advice of men who have no brains and do not know what they are talking about. Most small businessmen say simply, "Look at me." They fancy that if they have accumulated a little money and have got a position in a small circle, they are competent to give advice to anyone.

Next [in importance] to occupation is the building up of good taste. That is difficult, slow work. Few achieve it. It means all the difference in the world.

Joel Chandler Harris

―――

Coming into One's Own

Born in rural, mid-nineteenth-century Georgia, Joel Chandler Harris became famous for his Uncle Remus stories, recounting the adventures of animal characters like Brer Rabbit, Brer Fox, Brer Bear, and Brer Wolf. Originally trained as a painter and journalist during the plantation era, Harris was among the first American writers to use African-American dialect effectively.

Harris had six children, two of whom died of illness in their early years. In 1890, he encouraged his fifteen-year-old son, Julian, to visit his maternal grandparents in French Canada for several months. Father and son exchanged frequent letters that year. Here is one filled with tender sentiments about learning and choosing a career that Julian received in November:

> You ought to jot down in your notebook the words and phrases of patois that you hear—the speech of the common

people. They will be of immense importance to you hereafter if you should dabble in literature, and they will be interesting if you should not.... Make notes of what you see and hear—the thousand and one little intimations and suggestions that float in the air.

Another thing—when I make a remark or a suggestion, don't take it too seriously. You are old enough to have discovered, or at least, to have suspected that, except in the matter of morals, it is impossible to map out a young man's career by means of advice. All that I can do is to give you some of the results of my own experience.... I should like to see you with a will strong enough to resist all forms of temptation. Your career will then take care of itself.... You have individuality enough to make your impress on the public in various ways, and when you get a little older, you will know which way to choose.

The Earl of Chesterfield

―――

Developing a Sociable Demeanor

The Fourth Earl of Chesterfield, Philip Dormer Stanhope, was an influential aristocrat and political figure in eighteenth-century England. While serving as ambassador in the Netherlands, he had an affair with a French governess and sired an out-of-wedlock son, Philip. When the lad was five years old, Lord Chesterfield began to correspond with him, offering witty and frank advice about how to be a gentleman. Over four hundred of these letters have survived, and comprise the earl's chief historical legacy today. In March 1747, he offered Philip this somewhat cynical guidance:

> An engaging, insinuating manner, an easy good breeding, a genteel behavior and address, are of infinitely more advantage than they are generally thought to be, especially here in England.
> Virtue and learning, like gold, have their intrinsic value; but if they are not polished, they certainly lose a great deal of their

lustre; and even polished brass will pass upon more people than rough gold. . . . What a number of sins does the cheerful, easy good breeding of the French frequently cover! Many of them want common sense, many more common learning; but in general, they make up so much by their manner for those defects that, frequently, they pass unnoticed. . . .

You know what virtue is; you may have it if you will. It is in every man's power, and miserable is [he] who has it not. Good sense God has given you. Learning you already possess. . . . With this, you are thrown out early into the world, where it will be your own fault if you do not acquire all the other accomplishments necessary to complete and adorn your nature.

Frank Nixon and his son Richard

―――

Developing Skill as a Debater

In later life, Richard Nixon often referred to his mother, Hannah, as having been a "remarkable woman" and even a "saint." He never made comparable remarks about his father, Frank, who had been a quick-tempered streetcar motorman before opening a service station, and finally a grocery store, in rural Southern California. Yet Frank Nixon had several key character traits that greatly influenced his ambitious son. Decades later, the former United States president recalled:

My father had an Irish quickness both to anger and to mirth. It was his temper that impressed me as a small child. He had temptestuous arguments with my brothers Harold and Don, and their shouting could be heard all through the neighborhood. He was a strict and stern disciplinarian, and I tried to follow my mother's example of not crossing him when he was in a bad mood. Perhaps my own aversion to personal confrontation dates back to these early recollections.

He often argued vehemently on almost any subject with the customers he waited on in the store. His outbursts were not personal; they were just his way of putting life into a discussion. . . . Whatever talent I have as a debater must have been acquired from my father, from his love of argument and disputation. When I was on the debating team in college, he would often drive me to the debates and sit in the back of the room listening intently. On the way home, he would dissect and analyze each of the arguments.

Frank Nixon's interest in politics made him an enthusiastic follower of his son's career from its very beginnings. Richard Nixon reminisced:

My success meant to him that everything he had worked for and believed in was true; that in America, with hard work and determination a man can achieve anything. During the years I was in Congress, I sent home copies of the daily *Congressional Record*. He read them cover to cover—something that no congressman or senator I knew ever took the time to do. When I was running for vice president, he wrote a typically straightforward letter to one of the newspapers he had read years before, suggesting that it support me: "This boy is one of five that I raised and they are the finest, I think, in the United States. If you care to give him a lift, I would say the *Ohio State Journal* is still doing some good."

Claude Aristide and his grandson
Jean-Bertrand

━━━

Developing Youthful Character

On February 7, 1991, at the age of thirty-seven, parish priest Jean-Bertrand Aristide was sworn in as Haiti's first democratically elected president. For a land long ravaged by corruption and brutality, the future finally seemed hopeful. But within less than a year, a military junta ousted Aristide. Eventually, the United States restored a democratic government in Haiti through the use of force.

Jean-Bertrand Aristide was born in Port-Salut, in the southwestern part of Haiti. His father died soon after his birth and the family emigrated to the capital. But they often returned to stay with Jean-Bertrand's maternal grandfather, who had an inspiring influence on the growing boy. "Whatever I am, influenced by so many admirable men and women, I owe the most to him," Haiti's leader recently reminisced:

This respected man played the role of justice of the peace. . . . He wanted to be certain that everyone in the hills of Port-Salut ate at least once a day. This humanist was revolted by injustice, whether of birth or of life. The word *justice* was constantly on his lips. . . .

My grandfather did not know how to read or write, but he exposed moral and transcendental values better than the greatest books. His love for others shone in his eyes when he let fly at me, while shaving himself in the morning: "You cannot count the hairs in my beard, but you can count the people here who are suffering from injustice."

Every summer, I returned to Port-Salut. My grandfather showed me his gardens with great passion, insisting that everyone should work and sacrifice to make the land fruitful: a land that everyone had ardently cultivated and whose fruits everyone, whether an owner or not, could share according to his or her needs. . . . It was as if my grandfather was trying to make me remember at every moment that, no matter how poor, every person is a human being.

Thomas Jefferson

―――

Apply Yourself

In 1782, when he was thirty-nine, Thomas Jefferson became a widower, responsible for raising two daughters, Martha ("Patsy") and Maria ("Polly"). Grief-stricken and lonely at Monticello, he gladly accepted a congressional position to serve his country as an emissary to the French court. Later, Jefferson would accept a place in George Washington's cabinet and serve two terms as president of the United States.

In 1784, Jefferson took his older daughter, eight-year-old Patsy, to Paris with him. Jefferson was intensely protective of her well-being. Perhaps feeling guilty while away in Aix-en-Provence in March 1785, he offered Patsy this heartfelt advice:

> It is your future happiness which interests me, and nothing can contribute more to it . . . than contracting a habit of industry and activity. Of all the cancers of human happiness, none cor-

rodes it with so silent, yet so baneful a tooth, as indolence. Body and mind both unemployed, our being becomes a burden, and every object about us loathsome, even the dearest. . . . Exercise and application produce order in our affairs, health of body, cheerfulness of mind, and these make us precious to our friends.

It is while we are young that the habit of industry is formed. If not then, it never is afterwards. The fortune of our lives therefore depends on employing well the short period of youth. If at any moment, my dear, you catch yourself in idleness, start from it as you would from a gulf. . . .

We are always equal to what we undertake with resolution. . . . It is part of the American character to consider nothing as desperate, to surmount every difficulty by resolution and contrivance. . . . My expectations for you are high; yet not higher than you may attain. Nobody in this world can make me so happy, or so miserable, as you.

Judge Lemuel Shaw

———

Finding Motivation

In mid-nineteenth-century New England, Judge Lemuel Shaw was a renowned lawyer, jurist, public servant, and social activist. Chief justice of the Massachusetts Supreme Court, Shaw was also prominent in the literary world—he was an influential friend of philosopher Ralph Waldo Emerson, and later became novelist Herman Melville's father-in-law.

Known for his uncompromising integrity, in 1840 Judge Shaw offered this stern advice to his teenage son Lemuel, who was having difficulty becoming motivated in boarding school:

> Your own welfare here and hereafter, in this life and in the life to come, depends upon the character you may form in your youth, depends upon your education. . . . And by the blessing of God, we mean to adopt such a concern as in our judgment, will

be best calculated to promote your good, whether it is the most agreeable at that time or not.

You will soon arrive at years of manhood to take your place in the world, and to stand or fall by your own merits and qualifications. If in the meantime you have established a good character, if you have formed and cherished pious and devout sentiments, a love of God, and feelings of kindness and benevolence to all mankind ... you may be useful, honorable, and happy. You will have the prospect of enjoying all the blessings which this life can afford.... But if your youth is wasted on trifling amusements, and mere temporary pleasures, you will fall into habits of indolence, perhaps of vice, and become a useless if not a pernicious member of society.

Now, you have an opportunity to acquire good habits, by industry, determination, and perseverence. There is no obstacle which at your time of life good resolution cannot overcome. You have now the means in your power. You have friends able and willing to help you.... Save the present moment, then take advantage of the present time.

King James I

—

Growing Into Duty

After the death of Queen Elizabeth, King James VI of Scotland inherited the English throne to become King James I. He belonged to the House of Stuart, which had ruled Scotland for more than two centuries. Crafty and dictatorial, James would prove to be an unpopular, authoritarian ruler.

On April 4, 1603, James sent this farewell letter to his oldest son, Prince Henry Frederick. Left at Stirling Castle with his Danish mother, the lad was nine years old and soon would become the Prince of Wales:

> My son, that I see you not before my parting, impute it to this great occasion wherein time is so precious; but that shall by God's grace shortly be recompensed by your coming to me shortly, and continued residence with me ever after. Let not this news make you proud or insolent, for a king's son and heir were you before.

The augmentation that is likely to fall on you is but in cares and heavy burdens.

Be therefore merry but not insolent ... keep your kindness but in honorable sort; choose none to be your playfellows but them that are wellborn; and above all things, give never good countenance to any but according as you shall be informed that they are in estimation with me.

Look upon all Englishmen that shall come to visit you as loving subjects, not with that ceremony as toward strangers, and yet with such heartiness as at this time they deserve.... Be diligent and earnest in your studies, that at your meeting with me I may praise you for your progress in learning. Be obedient to your master ... and procure my thanks, for in reverencing him you obey me and honor yourself.

Washington Irving

―――

Don't Rush into Marriage

Washington Irving was one of the first American authors to win respect in Europe as well as in the United States. His humorous, best-known stories were "Rip Van Winkle" and "The Legend of Sleepy Hollow." Born in New York City during the Revolutionary War, Irving was originally trained as a lawyer, but changed his career to become a writer. He spent many years living in Europe and, in later life, served as a United States diplomat to Spain.

Irving's fiancée died just before they were to marry. Heartbroken, he never married or had children of his own, but very much enjoyed being an uncle. Throughout his life, he often visited and corresponded with his many nieces and nephews. In May 1829, after traveling through Spain with his nephew Edgar, Irving offered him this cautionary advice about youthfulness, and especially romance:

Do not waste much time in mere pleasure and gallanting.

I would again caution you, as I once did verbally, against what is a common custom in our country—against heedlessly getting yourself entangled in any matrimonial engagement before you have the means or certain prospect of maintaining a family. I speak thus to you now, because I trust your heart is free from any particular attachment.

I know that when a young man is once in love, he is not expected to act any more with prudence or discretion. He must then marry in defiance of penury and starvation. Novels and romances have established sound doctrine on this head which is not to be controverted.

But believe me, a young man who marries early, without certain and easy means of subsistence, is half extinguished. All his talents and industry, which might otherwise have been freely exercised to their full scope and might have led him to fortune or distinction, must be immediately turned into the limited, anxious, and incessant struggle for mere daily bread. The romance of love soon vanishes in such a struggle.

Leopold Mozart and his son Wolfgang

The Risk of Infatuation

Leopold Mozart was a poor Salzburg musician, seemingly condemned to a respectable but limited career in a minor court. It is not surprising that he viewed little Wolfgang Amadeus's amazing musical ability as nothing less than a miracle from God—an enormous talent that he, as the boy's father, was meant to shepherd.

Leopold exerted a domineering influence throughout Wolfgang Amadeus's early life, until finally, at the age of twenty-two, Wolfgang fell in love with the sixteen-year-old court singer Aloysia Weber. Young Mozart announced to his father his immediate intention to marry Aloysia, promote her career, and raise a family with her.

Worried that his genius son might throw away his talent for a mere infatuation (and in so doing, ruin his parents financially), Leopold warned that Wolfgang could well end up in a garret filled with starving children. In a letter penned in February 1778, he sharply advised:

Your desire to help the oppressed you have inherited from your father. But you must really consider first of all the welfare of your parents, or else your soul will go to the devil. Think of me as you saw me when you left us, standing beside the carriage in a state of utter wretchedness. Ill as I was, I had been packing for you until two o'clock in the morning, and there I was at the carriage again at six o'clock, seeing to everything for you. Hurt me now, if you can be so cruel! Win fame and make money in Paris, then when you have money to spend, go off to Italy and get commissions for operas.

Mozart may not have liked his father's advice, but Aloysia eventually rejected him in favor of another suitor. Four years later, after an ardent courtship, Mozart married her sister Constanze.

Jorge Guillermo Borges and his son Jorge Luis Borges

Encouraging Learning

Argentina's Nobel Prize–winning writer was born in a Buenos Aires suburb in 1899. Throughout his life, he spoke reverentially of how his father, Jorge Guillermo Borges, a civil service attorney and part-time psychology teacher and writer, had inspired him.

"My father was very intelligent and, like all intelligent men, very kind," the younger Borges reminisced in later life. "Once, he told me that I should take a good look at soldiers, uniforms, barracks, flags, churches, priests, and butcher shops, since all these things were about to disappear, and I could tell my children that I had actually seen them. The prophecy has not yet come true, unfortunately. My father was such a modest man that he would have liked being invisible. . . . His idols were Shelley, Keats, and Swinburne. As a reader, he had two interests. First, books on metaphysics and psychology. . . . Second,

A MINE OF INFORMATION.

"What's a Centaur Papa?"

"A Centaur, my Child, is a Fabulous Creature, *now extinct!*"

literature and books about the East. It was he who revealed the power of poetry to me—the fact that words are not only a means of communication but also magic symbols and music."

When interviewed about the influence of his early years, Borges was emphatic, "The chief event in my life . . . was my father's library. In fact, I sometimes think that I have never strayed outside that library. I can still picture it. It was in a room of its own, with glass-fronted shelves, and must have contained several thousand volumes. Being so nearsighted, I have forgotten most of the faces of that time . . . and yet I vividly remember so many of the steel engravings in *Chambers' Encyclopedia* and in the *Britannica*."

In particular, Borges acquired his father's love for reading English poetry aloud and for immersing himself in dictionaries and encyclopedias. Two of his most celebrated stories offer surrealist, enigmatic images of encyclopedias and libraries.

When Jorge was six years old, he proudly announced to his father, "When I grow up, I'm going to be a writer." His first stories were nonsensical and mostly involved childish renderings of classics like those by Cervantes. But as the Nobel Prizewinner recalled admiringly, "My father never interfered. He wanted me to commit all my own mistakes, and once said, 'Children educate their parents, not the other way around.'"

Christian Bohr and his son Niels

———

Discovering Truth

The Danish physicist Niels Bohr, whose Nobel Prize–winning research on the atom revolutionized modern science, traced his accomplishments directly to his father's influence. A professor of physiology at the University of Copenhagen, Christian Bohr was admired for his research achievements and much more. He was one of the key figures around whom the city's intellectual and cultural life revolved.

When he was seven years old, Niels began elementary school, but found it hard to separate emotionally from his younger brother Harold. In a woodworking class, Niels began making a puppet theater for Harold and became heartbroken when told he could not take his handiwork home to finish it. To remedy the situation, Professor Bohr built a workbench for the two boys and equipped it with tools that he taught them to use. Before long, Niels had built another puppet theater for Harold. As the boys grew older, their father added a lathe to the workbench, and Niels, adept at working with his hands, acquired a skill in metalworking that stayed with him, most usefully, all his life.

Through his father, Niels Bohr developed a love for world culture and literature, especially Shakespeare and Dickens and Goethe. He was encouraged to recite whole sections of *Faust* from memory. Professor Bohr would often invite scientists as well as literary figures home for dinner and allow the children to sit and listen to their wide-ranging conversations about the world and nature. Niels later recalled these informal conversations as crucial to his creative mental development.

In his laboratory, the elder Bohr kept this verse by Goethe posted on a wall. Its optimistic theme about discovering truth would inspire Niels throughout his adult life:

> With the world and life expanded,
> Long years striving as demanded,
> Always searching, always grounded,
> Never closed off, often rounded,
> Saved in age by being true,
> Friendly, ready for the new,
> Mind serene and pure of purpose:
> Now, one surely will make progress.

Joseph Alsop Sr. and his son Joseph Jr.

Reading for Children

From Franklin D. Roosevelt's New Deal until the Vietnam War, Joseph Alsop (Jr.) was one of America's most influential and accomplished journalists. At the age of twenty-seven, Alsop started writing a nationally syndicated column from Washington, D.C. Over the years, he became a fixture in the capital's power structure, as well as a world traveler.

Alsop grew up in a well-connected New England family, related to both Franklin and Theodore Roosevelt. His parents' seven-hundred-acre estate in rural Avon, Connecticut, boasted a cook, a handyman, two maids, and a nurse to keep things running smoothly. Looking back years later, Alsop cherished not his early social standing or wealth, but his father's personal emphasis on education.

"[He] must have been one of only two or three men with college degrees among the Avon voters in my boyhood," Alsop recalled. "In the latter part of his life, when Father had dropped all other political activities, he served as first selectman of the town. . . . He insisted upon giving absolute priority to adequate teachers' salaries instead of spending on grander school buildings and other less-than-direct investments in education. As a result, the Avon school system had one of the best records among rural communities in Connecticut—for good teachers, after all, are what chiefly matter.

"My Father read to his children every evening for half an hour or more before dressing for dinner—and with surprising dramatic emphasis for so unstagy a man. With Father, we successively got through *The Wind in the Willows*, Lewis Carroll's *Alice* books and *The Hunting of the Snark* (from which I can still quote), followed by large doses of Kipling. A good deal more followed, including several former classics now in obscurity. . . . Thus my father had the principal responsibility for making reading the main private refuge of all his children."

Franklin Warren and his son Robert

—

Taking Questions Seriously

Robert Penn Warren grew up in the American South in the early decades of the twentieth century. He became a major poet, novelist, and literary critic. In 1947 he won the Pulitzer Prize for *All the King's Men,* a novel that artfully describes the rise and fall of a ruthless Southern politician. Later he won two more Pulitzer Prizes—both for poetry—and in the mid-1980s served as the first poet laureate of the United States.

Warren's father, Franklin, inspired a love for learning in his children and served for many years on his Kentucky town's school board. A successful banker, who in early life had wanted to be a writer, he often stressed to Robert that "Education is the only salvation for democracy," and nurtured his youngsters' scholastic interests by buying them special books and scientific equipment and arranging private academic lessons and far-off trips to parks and zoos. Shortly before

Warren's death in 1989, he wrote *Portrait of a Father*, which included this homage:

> At home, life was so perfectly organized that then I did not realize that it was organized at all. In the evenings of the early years, one parent read to a child, or children, while the other was occupied by a book or magazine. Later, when I was in school, our mother read to the smaller children while our father read to me. One matter in this regard stands out in my memory: the serious and never condescending way a question from one of us would be treated.
>
> For instance, after the reading from the history of Greece and then of Rome in the same series, I asked my father "whose side" should you be on in a history book. He seriously considered the question, said that it was a real question, and after a moment added that, as far as he could see, "you might try to be on the side of the people you were at the time reading about."
>
> That satisfied me then, and I suppose that, in a sense, it still does.

Alfred Adler

___

Encouraging Self-Esteem

Along with Sigmund Freud and Carl Jung, the Austrian physician Alfred Adler is ranked as a cofounder of modern psychotherapy. He emigrated to the United States in the mid-1920s and became a best-selling author and lecturer about child psychology, parenting, and family relations. Adler, who coined the phrase "inferiority complex," stressed that all youngsters need encouragement to develop healthy self-esteem. Two of Adler's four children, Alexandra and Kurt, followed in his footsteps to become psychiatrists. They greatly admired their warm, charismatic father and in later life told many anecdotes about him.

When Alexandra was ten years old, she experienced great difficulty with mathematics. "I actually skipped the first test and went home because I felt I couldn't do it," she recalled decades later.

"My father said, 'What is it? Do you really think those stupid things that everyone else can do, *you* can't do? If you try, you can do all of it.'"

After receiving her father's encouragement, Alexandra recalled, "In a very short time, I became the best in mathematics. My teacher told me, 'You see, Adler, if you try, you can do it.'"

During the same period, Kurt was having problems in the second grade. "My father was not at all impressed with the teachers we had, although we went to a so-called progressive school," Kurt recalled. One day, Kurt's teacher ridiculed him before the entire class about his lack of ability.

That evening, after telling his father about the episode, the lad was startled to hear the unexpected reply, "Your teacher is an idiot." Decades later, Kurt would still smile in relating how that pithy comment had bolstered his scholastic self-esteem.

But like nearly all educated men of his generation, Alfred Adler (as well as Sigmund Freud) found it almost impossible to discuss sex with his own children. He could write countless articles and books about its importance as a human drive, but with his own flesh and blood, matters were different. Only once in Adler's life with his only son, Kurt, did he even allude to sexuality.

In the mid-1920s, when an excited Kurt was about to leave on a high school graduation trip to Italy with a chum, his father called him into his study. "Remember, Kurt," he advised rather elliptically, "There is only one sure way to avoid venereal disease, and that is love."

King David

———

Faith in God

King David is one of the most beloved figures in Jewish history. According to tradition, he ruled for forty years after the death of his bitter foe Saul, the Israelites' first king. Recent archaeological evidence has increasingly substantiated David's reign in approximately the eleventh century B.C.E. The Hebrew Bible relates that several of his sons plotted and struggled among themselves to determine who would succeed him. Much to David's grief, his son Absalom was killed by royal soldiers in an unsuccessful revolt against the regime.

According to Chronicles I, at the end of King David's life, he gathered in Jerusalem all his advisors, stewards, seasoned warriors, and high officials, in order to publicly transfer rulership (on divine command) of Israel to his fourteen-year-old son, Solomon, and to announce a temple was to be built there.

WILLING TO OBLIGE.

Uncle (to little Bertie, aged five, who is being taken off to bed). "Good night, Bertie. Of course you always remember your aunts and uncles in your prayers?"

Bertie. "Oh yes, Uncle Felix. Shall I tell you what I say? I say, 'God bless Aunty Kitty, and make her thin; and God bless Uncle James, and make him fat; and God bless Uncle Felix, and—,' which do you want to be—fat or thin?"

These were David's fatherly words in front of the entire assemblage:

And you, Solomon, my son, know the God of your father, and serve him with a whole heart and with a willing mind; for the Lord searches all hearts, and understands every plan and thought. If you seek him, he will be found by you; but if you forsake him, he will cast you off forever. Take heed now, for the Lord has chosen you to build a house for the sanctuary; be strong, and do it.

Thereupon, after presenting to Solomon the detailed, divinely inspired plan for the temple, David further advised his loyal son:

Be strong and of good courage, and do it. Fear not, be not dismayed; for the Lord God, even my God, is with you. He will not fail you or forsake you, until all the work for the service of the house of the Lord is finished. And behold the divisions of the priests and the Levites for all the service of the house of God; and with you in all the work will be every willing man who has skill for any kind of service; and also the officers and all the people will be totally at your command.

The Bible recounts "All the assembly blessed the Lord and they made Solomon, the son of David, king."

Lukman

The Importance of Humility

According to Islamic tradition, the seventh-century prophet Muhammad received the Koran through revelation over many years. These revelations were subsequently written down by Muhammad's followers, until the Koran's standard text emerged about twenty years after his death in the year 632.

Composed of verses grouped into chapters of considerably varying length, the Koran has been taught orally and is memorized, at least in part, by virtually all Islamic adherents. Its thirty-first chapter, devoted to a holy man known as Lukman, includes this advice to his son:

> O my son! Offer prayers perfectly, enjoin people for Islamic monotheism and all that is good, and forbid people from disbelief is the oneness of Allah, polytheism of all kinds and all that is evil and bad, and bear with patience whatever befalls you.

Verily! These are some of the commandments ordered by Allah with no exemption:

Turn not your face away from men with pride, nor walk in insolence through the earth. Verily, Allah likes not each arrogant boaster.

Be moderate or show no insolence in your walking, and lower your voice. Verily, the harshest of all voices is the braying of the ass.

See you not that Allah has subjected for you whatsoever is in the heavens and whatsoever is in the earth, and has completed and perfected His graces for you, both the apparent and the lawful pleasures of the world, and also the delights of the hereafter in Paradise?

And to Allah return all matters for decision.

Moses

━━━

A Continuing Faith

Clearly, Moses is one of the most important figures of the Hebrew Bible. Yet, curiously, the Israelites' great liberator from Egyptian slavery and subsequent law-giver is rarely acknowledged as a father. The bible does not even mention the names of his offspring, though later Hebrew legends arose about them.

But in a larger sense, Moses is portrayed as father of his people, who are described consistently as "the children of Israel." As narrated in Deuteronomy, Moses received a final divine instruction: that before he was to die overlooking the Promised Land, he was to gather the twelve tribes and bless each of them. According to tradition, this public ceremony was designed to insure for his generation—and for all future generations—a continuing faith in their divine mission and purpose:

> "Let Reuben live, and not die,
>   nor let his men be few."

And this he said of Judah:
"Hear, O Lord, in the voice of Judah,
    and bring him to his people.
With thy hands contend for him,
    and be a help against his
        adversaries."

And of Levi he said,
"Give to Levi thy Thummim,
    and thy Urim to thy godly one,
whom they didst test at Massah,
    with whom thou didst strive at the
        waters of Meribah;
who said of his father and mother
    'I regard them not';
he disowned his brothers,
    and ignored his children.
For they observed thy word,
    and kept thy covenant.
They shall teach Jacob thy
        ordinances,
    and Israel thy law;
they shall put incense before thee,
    and whole burnt offerings upon thy
        altar.

Bless, O Lord, his substance,
   and accept the work of his hands;
crush the loins of his adversaries,
   of those that hate him, that they
      rise not again."

Of Benjamin he said,
"The beloved of the Lord,
   he dwells in safety by him;
he encompasses him all the day long,
   and makes his dwelling between
      his shoulders."

And of Joseph he said,
"Blessed by the Lord be his land,
   with the choicest gifts of heaven
      above,
   and of the deep that couches
      beneath,
with the choicest fruits of the sun,
   and the rich yield of the months,
with the finest produce of the ancient
      mountains,
   and the abundance of the
      everlasting hills,

with the best gifts of the earth and
its fullness,
and the favor of him that dwelt
in the bush.
Let these come upon the head of
Joseph,
and upon the crown of the head
of him that is prince among his
brothers.
His firstling bull has majesty,
and his horns are the horns of a
wild ox;
with them he shall push the peoples,
all of them, to the ends of the
earth;
such are the ten thousands of
Ephraim,
and such are the thousands of
Manasseh."

And of Zebulun he said,
"Rejoice, Zebulun, in your going out;
and Isachar, in your tents.
They shall call peoples to their
mountain;

there they offer right sacrifices;
for they suck the affluence of the seas
    and the hidden treasures of the sand."

And of Gad he said,
"Blessed be he who enlarges Gad!
    Gad couches like a lion,
    he tears the arm, and the crown
      of the head.
He chose the best of the land for himself,
    for there a commander's portion
      was reserved:
and he came to the heads of the
      people,
    with Israel he executed the
      commands
    and just decrees of the Lord."

And of Dan he said,
"Dan is a lion's whelp,
    that leaps forth from Bashan."

And of Naphtali he said,
"O Napthali, satisfied with favor,
    and full of the blessing of the Lord,
    possess thou the lake and the south."

And of Asher he said,
"Blessed above sons be Asher;
   let him be the favorite of his
      brothers,
   and let him dip his foot in oil.
Your bars shall be iron and bronze;
   and as your days, so shall your
      strength be."

After blessing the twelve tribes in this manner, Moses praised and thanked God once more. He ended his farewell ceremony with these words: "Happy are you, O Israel! Who is like you, a people saved by the Lord, the shield of your help and the sword of your triumph!"

John Muir

━━

Religion and Nature

John Muir was one of the greatest explorers and naturalists in American history. An eloquent writer who extolled nature's grandeur, he inspired the early conservation movement in this country. Muir also possessed strong faith and viewed his calling in almost religious terms. Among his many accomplishments, in 1890 he effectively influenced Congress to pass the Yosemite National Park Act, establishing both Yosemite and Sequoia national parks.

Throughout John Muir's colorful life, he enjoyed tramping around the globe, including North America, Europe, Africa, and even the Arctic. Often his wife and two daughters would join him on local expeditions. While exploring his beloved native Scotland in July 1893, Muir offered these religious sentiments to his twelve-year-old daughter, Annie Wanda, back home:

I suppose you are now a big girl, almost a woman, and you must mind your lessons and get in a good store of the best words of the best people while your memory is retentive, and then you'll go through the world rich.

Ask mother to give you lessons to commit to memory every day. Mostly the sayings of Christ in the gospels and selections from the poets. Find the hymn of praise in *Paradise Lost,* "These are thy glorious works, Parent of Good, Almighty," and learn it well.

Last evening, I took a walk along the shore on the rocks where I played when a boy. The waves made a grand show, breaking in sheets and sheaves of foam, and grand songs—the same old songs they sang to me in my childhood—and I seemed a boy again, and all the long eventful years in America were forgotten while I was filled with that glorious ocean psalm.

Isaac Bashevis Singer

———

Faith and a Secular Life

Born in Poland, Isaac Bashevis Singer emigrated to the United States before World War II. In 1978 he won the Nobel Prize for literature in recognition of his masterful short stories and novels. Among his best-known works are *Satan in Goray, The Magician of Lublin, Yentl,* and *The Spinoza of Market Street.* Writing in Yiddish, he created memorable characters who struggled with religious, moral, and sexual impulses to find meaning in human life.

When he emigrated from Warsaw several years before the Nazi invasion, Singer left behind his first wife and five-year-old son, Israel. More than twenty years passed before father and son met again in New York City, but the two gradually became close. As Isaac Bashevis Singer gained international fame, he often traveled to visit his son, who'd settled in Israel, and enjoyed the role of a doting grandfather there.

In the summer of 1986, Israel spent a good deal of time visiting his ailing father in New York City. "How can a person like you claim to believe in God, yet live a completely secular life?" he asked in bewilderment. This was his father's ironic but forceful reply:

Can you explain the world without God? Whenever I'm in trouble, I look up in the sky and pray. Since I'm in trouble most of the time, I never stop praying. Not a regular prayer from the prayer book. A personal conversation between me and the Creator. Mostly I plead with Him, but sometimes I also complain. I often told Him that I don't justify His acts. Not a day goes by without a sharp dialogue between us.

In many cases, He responds to my prayers and gives answers to my distress. Sometimes the plot of my story is stuck like a cart in the mud, and I don't know how to get it out. I prostrate myself, hesitate, sometimes put in a prayer to Him, and suddenly a heavenly illumination, and the cart slides out of the swampy mud.

The belief that man is master of his fate is as far from me as east is from west. God is silent, speaks in acts; and we on earth have to decipher His secrets. . . . Our great hope is free choice, a divine gift.

David Goodman and his son Benny

A Father's Devotion

Benny Goodman, the celebrated bandleader and clarinetist known as the King of Swing, was the son of poor Eastern European Jewish immigrants. His parents, David and Dora, met in Baltimore, then moved to Chicago where they raised twelve children. Their ninth was Benny. Benny's father worked as a tailor, putting in ten-to-fourteen-hour days to support the family.

While Dora fed and cared for her growing brood at home, David Goodman did most of the grocery shopping, took the children to buy shoes and trousers when there was enough money, and pressed them about the importance of education. His famous son Benny later recalled:

"Pop was always trying to get us to study, so that we would get ahead in the world. He always envied people with book-learning and education. Whatever any of us have amounted to may be pretty much traced to him."

It was the elder Goodman who encouraged Benny to play an instrument, after discovering that the local synagogue had a boys' band, provided lessons, and offered inexpensive rentals of musical instruments. According to family legend, his older brother Harry was given a tuba because he was the biggest; next-in-size Freddy played a trumpet, and ten-year-old Benny, the smallest of the three, a clarinet.

By the time he was eighteen, in 1927, Benny Goodman was so successful as a musician that his father was able to quit working as a tailor. David Goodman had no interest in being idle, however, and declared he wanted to own a newsstand. When Benny protested, telling his father, "There's plenty of money coming in now, you don't need to work anymore," the older man looked him in the eye and said, "Benny, you take of yourself, I'll take care of myself."

David Goodman was killed in a streetcar accident not long afterward, and Benny always regretted that his devoted father never received an appropriate reward for his years of toil. As a close friend later recalled, "[Benny] reminisced about his dad at times, and tears would come into his eyes. Dad encouraged them—a very kind man, very poor man. Dad wanted the kids to have everything."

Chief Joseph (Tuekakas) and his son Chief Joseph the Younger

━━━━

Honoring Your People

With remarkable dignity, determination, and dedication to the cause of his people, Chief Joseph the Younger of the Nez Percé tribe was respected in his time as a Native American leader and spokesperson. In 1877 he reluctantly went to war against invading settlers who demanded that his tribe move from their Oregon valley homeland. After skirmishes and fierce battle, Chief Joseph finally surrendered.

In April 1879, the *North American Review* published his speech entitled, "An Indian's View of Indian Affairs." In it, Chief Joseph related how his own father—the previous chief—had inspired him to keep alive their tribe's continuing struggle for freedom. These were his dying father's final words:

My son, my body is returning to my mother earth, and my spirit is going very soon to see the Great Spirit Chief. When I am gone, think of your country. You are the chief of these people. They look to you to guide them. Always remember that your father never sold this country. You must stop your ears whenever you are asked to sign a treaty selling your home. A few years more, and white men will be all around you. They have their eyes on this land. My son, never forget my dying words. This country holds your father's body. Never sell the bones of your father and your mother.

Nahmanides

―――

Learning Humility

Born in Gerona, Spain, about the year 1195, Nahmanides was one of the greatest rabbis in Jewish history. An erudite mystic, he presented Judaism from the vantage point of fervent feeling rather than of dry intellect. At the venerable age of seventy, Nahmanides emigrated to the Holy Land and there completed his most important work, a commentary on the Bible. At the same time, he embarked upon a historic mission: to revive the nearly extinguished medieval Jewish community in the Holy Land.

While living in Jerusalem during this period, Nahmanides wrote often to family members back in Spain. About the year 1270, he offered his adult son Nahman this inspiring advice about humility:

> Hear, my son, the instruction of your father, and forsake not the law of your mother. My son, my beloved, accustom yourself always to speak gently to everyone, at all times and seasons; and you shall thereby avoid anger, which is a very bad and blameworthy disposition.

When you avoid anger, you will bring to your mind the quality of humility, and cleave onto it, for it is the best of all virtues, as it is written: "The reward of humility is the fear of the Lord." Even our teacher Moses, peace be with him, was praised for this quality. It is by reason of this virtue that the Torah was given by his hand, and that he was called the teacher of all prophets. He who attains this quality is beloved of Heaven, as it is written: "I dwell in the high and holy place, with him that is of a contrite and humble spirit."

I now set forth for you how you should conduct yourself according to the quality of humility, to follow it continually. Let all your words be spoken with gentleness, with respect, with good manners, and with love. Your countenance should be pleasant, and your head bowed down. Your eyes should look downward, and your heart upward. Do not gaze too freely upon a man when you address him. Let everyone be greater than you in your sight. If he is rich, you shall honor him, as did our saintly teacher, who used to honor the rich. If he is poor and you are rich, you shall have mercy and compassion on him, and honor the Lord with your charity. If you are wiser than he, you should consider that you are guilty, and he is innocent.

In all your thoughts, words, and deeds, at all times and seasons, regard yourself as though you stood before the supreme King of Kings, the Holy One, blessed be He.

Vince Lombardi

―――

Learning from Your Mistakes

The famous coach of the Green Bay Packers football team is well remembered today for his aphorism, "Winning isn't just the main thing. Winning is *every*thing." He relentlessly drove the young athletes of the National Football League whom he coached brilliantly for decades. Lombardi was equally demanding at home with his two children, Vince Jr. and Susan.

Academically gifted Vince Jr. initially wanted to major in physical education in the hope of becoming a football coach, but his father objected, arguing that an easy phys-ed major was a waste of time for someone with his son's considerable intelligence. Besides, Lombardi bluntly told his son, "You don't want to do what I'm doing." Rather, Lombardi always encouraged Vince Jr. to be a lawyer, and when his son finally switched to prelaw and won an academic scholarship, Lombardi was delighted and proud.

Rigorous scholastic preparation would strengthen his son's mind and character, Lombardi reasoned; arduous summer work would build his character and body. Each summer, therefore, Lombardi carefully chose his son's jobs, which included heavy construction or loading boxes into semis. At the time, Vince Jr. chafed under his father's discipline, but years later conceded to an interviewer, "I don't feel any worse for [it]."

Susan was five years younger than Vince Jr. and more of an extrovert than her scholastically minded brother. Her father had mellowed slightly by the time Susan was growing up and did not push her quite as hard academically. Lombardi took time to help Susan with algebra and Latin, and enthusiastically encouraged her horseback riding and appearances in horse shows. They also spent time just talking together.

The piece of advice that Susan most fondly remembers from the man later dubbed "the winningest coach in history" was: "You'll make a lot of mistakes in life. But if you learn from every mistake, you really didn't make a mistake."

Warren Buffett

———

Learning the Value of Money

According to *Forbes* magazine, Warren Buffett is the second-richest man in the world today—surpassed only by his friend Bill Gates Jr. of Microsoft. Starting from scratch, inventing nothing, simply by picking stocks and companies for investment, Buffett has amassed one of the epochal fortunes of the twentieth century—an astounding net worth of ten billion dollars, and counting.

Intelligent and offbeat, Buffett has been described as possessing a dual personality when it comes to money: It means both nothing and everything to him. The Oracle of Omaha, as he's been called, has always preferred a modest lifestyle. His three children attended public school, and he encouraged them to do what they enjoyed, irrespective of what they would earn. In fact, his younger son Peter discovered the extent of their father's vast fortune only after reading about it in a newspaper.

A FAIR WARNING.

"Daddy, I want you to give me five shillings a week Pocket-money!"

"I couldn't do it, my little Chap. It's too much!"

"Well, I must have it. If you won't, I shall go and bet!"

His daughter Susie has recalled, "We didn't live any differently from anyone else. I could charge clothes and never get into trouble—that was the only difference. I didn't have a car. I had to get a job at sixteen—at the Carriage Shop, as a salesperson."

From their immensely wealthy father, the Buffett children specifically learned that money could be a tremendous motivator for self-improvement. Once, when Warren Buffett was trying to lose weight by dieting, he wrote an astonished little Susie a ten-thousand-dollar check, payable to her on such-and-such date, but added an "escape clause": *if his weight dropped, the check would become completely void.*

Susie tried plying her Midas-like father with ice cream and dragging him to McDonald's, but such tactics proved useless. He didn't want the ice cream as much as he wanted to keep the money.

Ernest Hemingway

━━━━

Handling Money

It was the summer of 1940, and Ernest Hemingway was at the peak of his fame. Living on an estate owned by the Union Pacific Railroad in Sun Valley, California, he was finishing his novel *For Whom the Bell Tolls*—and supervising his three sons. As the youngest child, at age nine, Gregory later recalled, "[It was] the first summer we spent with Papa after Mother divorced him . . . and the railroad could tell the world that he was there, and could take a reasonable number of pictures of the Hemingways at play. In return for this everything was on the house."

During his first month at Sun Valley, Gregory was left on his own a great deal of the time, and unknowingly ran up a huge expense tab. He had been ordering a big meal daily at the posh Ram Restaurant and then feeding much of the food to tame ducks living on the nearby pond. Decades later, in *Papa, a Personal Memoir*, Gregory recalled:

"Papa called me into his room. I was scared. Although he was always gentle with me, his size was intimidating.

"'Gig, I haven't taught you anything about the value of money. Basically, it's worthless, but it lets you buy a lot of things that you can enjoy. When you sign for things here, it's just like spending the nickels and dimes I give you for pocket money. We won't always have this much, so enjoy it while you can.

"'I'm not saying this will spoil you for good or permanently ruin your sense of values. You'll find out soon enough how difficult money is to come by and you'll shepherd what you have when you're older and can add.'

"Then Papa came to the point. 'That nice man, Mr. Anderson, the one who runs this place, is a little [angry],' Papa said. 'He says you've set some sort of record for a nine-year-old in one month. Even the Aga Khan's kid only spent two hundred dollars the month he was here." Papa laughed, then added, in a more serious voice, 'We might have to leave if you keep this up.'

"My face fell—who would feed the ducks?

"'Mr. Anderson didn't say we'd have to leave, but he asked me to talk to you. So try to keep the signing down. Don't order such fancy things and take it easy on the skeet and skating lessons. The pheasant and duck shooting will start soon and I'll take you out with us when we go. That, at least, will make up for the skeet shooting you'll miss. Live birds are more fun, anyway.

117

"'You can eat pretty much what you want but no more guinea hens under glass or that flaming meat on a stick. The swimming and bowling are okay, though, and you can fish and ride as much as you want. Just take it a little easier, pal. You certainly wouldn't want to embarrass the family and get us thrown out, would you?'

"So I cut down. The next month I lowered my bill to under three hundred dollars and although still less than delighted, Papa could always recognize improvement. It meant I could not only keep my friends the ducks, but protect my family from permanent disgrace."

George Lucas Sr. and his son George Jr.

The Wisdom of Saving

George Lucas (Jr.) is one of the most successful movie directors of all time. His box-office hits include *American Graffiti, Star Wars, The Empire Strikes Back*, and *Raiders of the Lost Ark*. He grew up in post–World War II California, and was especially drawn to fairy tales, comic books, and adventure shows on television.

George Lucas Sr. was a successful small-town merchant in quiet Modesto, California. A church-going Methodist, he believed in teaching his children the value of discipline and hard work. He started them on allowances at age four: four cents a week, with annual increases as they grew older. In later years, they had to perform various chores for this sum. George Sr. and his wife Dorothy had grown up during the Depression and weren't about to let their children forget that "money doesn't grow on trees." Even in later years, Lucas remarked that "Every generation should have to go through a Depression."

In the mid-1950s, at the age of eleven George Jr. had to mow the lawn each week to earn his allowance. The assignment wasn't arbitrary; it was a clear example of the work-reward principle. George Jr. didn't mind doing the work, but he was small and felt unable physically to perform the job well. "The frustrating thing was that it was tough grass to mow, and I was a little kid," he recalled decades later.

To get the work done and still satisfy his strict father, George Jr. developed a resourceful response. He saved his allowance every week for four months until he accumulated thirty-five dollars. Then he borrowed another twenty-five dollars from his mother (also repaid from his allowance) and bought his own sixty-dollar lawnmower.

George Sr. was initially furious, but then felt impressed by his son's boldness and ingenuity. As he probably realized, he had indeed taught the lad a valuable lesson about using his intelligence to triumph in a seemingly no-win situation.

Lewis Carroll

Learning to Be Responsible

The famous English author of *Alice's Adventures in Wonderland* (whose real name was Charles Dodgson) was a shy mathematics professor at Oxford and a deacon with strong moralistic sensitivities. His fantasies of magical queens and talking animals appealed tremendously to the Victorian imagination.

Though Dodgson never married or became a father, he loved the company of children. In this letter written in July 1895, the celebrated story-teller offered religious guidance to his teenage nephew Bertram Collingwood:

> I am sending you the article on "Eternal Punishment," as it is. There is plenty of matter for consideration, as to which I shall be glad to know your views.
>
> Also if there are other points, connected with religion, where you feel that perplexing difficulties exist, I should be glad to

know of them in order to see whether I can see my way to saying anything helpful.

But I had better add that I do not want to deal with any such difficulties, *unless* they tend to affect *life*. *Speculative* difficulties which do not affect conduct, and which come into collision with any of the principles which I intend to state as axioms, lie outside the scope of my book. These axioms are:

1. Human conduct is capable of being *right*, and of being *wrong*.

2. I possess Free-Will, and am able to choose between right and wrong.

3. I have in some cases chosen wrong.

4. I am responsible for choosing wrong.

5. I am responsible to a person.

6. This person is perfectly good.

I call them axioms, because I have no *proofs* to offer them. There will probably be others, but these are all I can think of just now.

Samuel Goldwyn

———

Loving Your Children

In the insular, gilded community of Hollywood's founding moguls, Samuel Goldwyn was regarded as unusually devoted to his family. Although he frequently gambled and womanized, his daily conduct seemed almost saintly by the standards of his peers. During one of Kennedy family patriarch Joseph P. Kennedy's occasional forays into Southern California's tinseltown, he remarked that Goldwyn was the only man in Hollywood "with a true family life."

Many years later, Sam Goldwyn Jr. recalled of his father, "My earliest memories are of him kissing me." He particularly remembered his fourth birthday, on September 7, 1930. At seven o'clock in the morning, Little Sammy, as he was affectionately known, tore down the stairs of the Goldwyns' two-story summer home.

"Daddy, I'm four years old!" he shrieked excitedly.

Already immersed in a high-stakes card game at that early hour,

Goldwyn Sr. halted him, saying, "Just a minute . . . till I finish this hand." A moment later, the famous movie producer furiously yelled, "Goddammit!" threw all his cards down, then swept his son into his arms and kissed him.

"Actually," amended Sam Goldwyn Jr. in reminiscing about this episode, "my earliest memories are all of my father playing cards."

Robert Browning

Marriage and Its Benefits

Robert Browning was one of the great poets of Victorian England. With paternal encouragement, he began reading avidly at the age of five. Spending countless hours browsing in his father's (Robert Browning Sr.) well-stocked library, which included books on painting and music, young Browning eventually decided to become a writer.

His wife was Elizabeth Barrett Browning, also greatly admired as a poet and essayist. Their only child was Robert Barrett ("Pen") Browning, who was a struggling and unsettled writer for many years. In August 1887, the elder, widowed Browning sent thirty-eight-year-old Pen this guidance about his imminent plans for marriage:

> I think you could not do a wiser, better thing than marry the in-every-way-suitable lady whom you have been fortunate enough to induce to take such a step, and who, you are bound to feel, behaves with the utmost generosity.

You know very well I have never had any other aim than your happiness in all I have done: The kind of life you have been forced to lead these last years always seemed comfortless and even dangerous to me—whatever might be said for it as helpful to your art (and *that* it no doubt was)—you must know that it had lasted long enough for the purpose, and could not, in the nature of things, continue as you advance in years: "No home"—is sad work. With a home, and *such* a home, as with *such* a wife as yours will be, your further progress will be infinitely more easy and rapid. I do approve of your choice with all my heart.

Franklin D. Roosevelt

———

Maximizing Your College Education

Franklin D. Roosevelt hadn't yet become governor of New York State or president of the United States when his first-born son James, at the age of nineteen, was beginning studies at Harvard. But, as a former vice presidential candidate, Roosevelt was already a national figure in the Democratic party.

In August 1926, he wrote this letter to Harvard's dean Chester Greenough and sent an advance copy to son James. It was likely written as much for him as for the dean.

> One of the principal troubles with most of these private-school undergraduates of yours is, I am convinced after a great deal of investigation, that their parents give them a great deal too much money to go through college on. To this is added in most cases, automobiles, and all sorts of expensive toys in the holidays. . . . I, as one graduate of many, want to cooperate with you in this.

During the past summer, my boy has worked as a laborer in a Canadian pulp and paper mill.

Concretely in regard to my boy, I feel the following should be the objectives:

1. Better scholarship than passing marks.

2. Athletics to be a secondary, not a primary objective.

3. Activity in student activities such as debating, *Crimson*, etc., to be encouraged.

4. Acquaintance with the average of the class, not just the Mt. Auburn Street crowd, to be emphasized.

5. Opportunity to earn part of his education.

Walter Raleigh

——

Use of Intellect

In the early decades of the twentieth century, Walter Raleigh was admired as an English educator and writer. Although he only lived to be forty-three years old, he produced many articles and several well-regarded books on Shakespeare, Wordsworth, literary style, and other related topics. With a witty outlook, his well-reasoned essays extolled the virtues of reading and original thinking.

In June 1920, Raleigh offered this advice to his daughter Philippa, who was complaining about college:

> If you use [your] intellect, you don't need to talk about it; you can put it across the talkers. The only thing good to study is something that catches you and excites you once you have given it a chance. I hope you will choose what you like best, and then you shall hear lectures or teachers who know and care about it.

The world is a curious and various place. The great thing to do in it is to be decent; anything else is mostly luck. Most of us get some chunks of luck, and the best of us are all right even if [we] don't.

Charles Dickens

Maxims for Success

As England's most famous writer of the nineteenth century, Charles Dickens enjoyed a huge and appreciative audience. His novels like *Oliver Twist* and *Great Expectations* often vividly portrayed children struggling for their place in an indifferent world. Dickens himself had ten children, and their problems consumed his attention throughout his life.

Accurately sensing that they would never meet again, a frail, aging Dickens offered this advice in September 1868 to his youngest son, eighteen-year-old Edward ("Plorn"), who was about to set sail for a new life in Australia:

> I need not tell you that I love you dearly, and am very, very sorry in my heart to part with you. But this life is half made up of partings, and these pains must be borne. It is my comfort and my sincere conviction that you are going to try the life for which you

are best fitted. I think its freedom and wildness more suited to you than any experiment in a study or office would ever have been, and without that training, you could have followed no other occupation. . . .

Never take a mean advantage of anyone in any transaction, and never be hard upon people who are in your power. Try to do to others, as you would have them do for you, and do not be discouraged if they fail sometimes. It is much better for you that that they should fail in obeying the greatest rule laid down by our Savior, than that you should. . . .

Only one more thing on this head. The more we are in earnest as to feeling it, the less we are disposed to hold forth about it. Never abandon the wholesome practice of saying your own private prayers, night and morning. I have never abandoned it myself, and I know the comfort of it.

I hope you will always be able to say in life, that you had a kind father.

Mahatma Gandhi

———

Essential Virtues

The father and inspirational leader of modern India was Mahatma Gandhi. In early adulthood, he spent much of his time in South Africa, whose rulers bitterly opposed his campaigns for racial equality and passive resistance there. While serving a prison term there in 1909, he wrote encouragingly to his son Manilal, back home in India.

The second of four children born to the Gandhis, Manilal had nearly died of typhoid when he was a child, and now, at seventeen, helped to support the family. In later life, Manilal, an editor and activist, worked closely with his world-respected father to spearhead India's independence movement against British rule.

How are you? Although I think that you are well able to bear all the burden I have placed on your shoulders and that you are doing it quite cheerfully, I have often felt that you required greater personal guidance than I have been able to give you. I know too that you have sometimes felt that your education was being neglected. Now I have read a good deal in the prison. I have been reading Emerson, Ruskin . . . and the Upanishads. All confirm the view that education does not mean a knowledge of letters but it means character building. It means a knowledge of duty.

Amusement only continues during the age of innocence, that is, up to twelve years only. As soon as a boy reaches the age of discretion, he is taught to realize his responsibilities. Every boy from such stage onward should practice *continence in thought and deed, truth likewise, and the not-taking of any life*. This to him must not be an irksome learning and practice, but it should be natural to him. It should be his enjoyment. I can recall to my mind several such boys in Rajkot.

Let me tell you that when I was younger than you are, my keenest enjoyment was to nurse my father. Of amusement after I was twelve, I had little or none. If you practice the three [above-mentioned] virtues, if they become part of your life, so far as I am concerned you will have completed your education—your training. Armed with them, believe me, you will earn your bread in any part of the world and you will have paved the way to acquire a true knowledge of the soul, yourself, and God.

Lorenzo de' Medici

Rising Early

The Spanish discovery of America by Christopher Columbus in 1492 was not the only remarkable event that year. Seven months earlier, a precocious lad of sixteen was being formally inducted as a member of the most exclusive of all Catholic religious groups—the College of Cardinals. The youth was Giovanni de' Medici, the second of the three sons of the wealthy banker Lorenzo, called "the Magnificent" by his admiring contemporaries. Through his efforts, Florence became the most powerful state in Italy and one of the world's most beautiful cities.

After participating in the ceremonies, Giovanni went to his lodging and found a letter from his powerful father. It contained the following advice:

> You are not only the youngest cardinal in the college, but the youngest person that was ever raised to that rank; and you ought

therefore to be the most vigilant and unassuming, not giving others occasion to wait for you. . . . You will soon get a sufficient insight into the manner of your brethren. With those of less respectable character converse not with too much intimacy; not merely on account of the circumstance in itself, but for the sake of public opinion. Converse on general topics with all. On public occasions, let your equipage and dress be below rather than above mediocrity. A handsome house and a well-ordered family will be preferable to a great retinue and a splendid residence.

Endeavor to live with regularity, and gradually to bring your expenses within those bounds which in a new establishment cannot perhaps be expected. Silk and jewels are not suitable for persons in your station. Your taste will be better shown in the acquisition of a few elegant remains of antiquity, or in the collecting of handsome books, and by your attendants being learned and well bred rather than numerous. Invite others to your house oftener than you receive invitations. Practice neither too frequently. . . .

There is one rule that I would recommend to your attention in preference to all others: Rise early in the morning. This will not only contribute to your health, but will enable you to arrange and expedite the business of the day, and as there are various duties incident to your station, such as the performance of divine service, studying, and giving audience, you will find the observance of this admonition productive of the greatest utility.

Martin of Padilla and Manrique

Governing Oneself

In the late sixteenth century, Spain, Europe's major power, faced shifting alliances and rivalries with England, France, and Turkey. The tradition-minded Spanish ruler, King Phillip II, was also involved in exerting military control over subordinate states. In 1580 he sent troops to maintain order in Portugal, and then, in 1591, to Granada.

It is against this historical backdrop that Martin of Padilla and Manrique, the mayor-governor of Castilia, offered guidance in May 1596 to his son Juan, who was beginning an active military career:

> Grateful am I that you have chosen such an honorable state, which can give you such greatness, if you govern yourself accordingly.
>
> Your first motive should be that your works and undertakings be for God, whom you shall always have present in all your actions, which will therefore be directed with great honor and advantage.
>
> To be liberal should have its proportion, so that it does not

become perdition. Neither are you to give all persons equally, but consider the needs and the obligations that you would have toward each of them.

Reflect often about the state of affairs and judge with discretion about what is to come. . . . Do not put your people in manifest dangers, and what you can accomplish with money, work, and wit do not complete with the loss of a single soldier.

For no reason at all become rich in a hurry, even if you can, because all violent things are transient, and they may take your honor, life, and soul.

The good soldier should always be exemplary in his life. Moreover, with much care you will become so when an officer. You will not be able to reprimand others for faults that you yourself have. You shall be comrades with the most valiant and virtuous, because they will respond with love and truth, and will not put you in shameful situations.

Be aware that there will be those who murmur against you, saying you are a hypocrite. What you do, do for God and do not cease your actions because of what people may say. Always forgive others through good means, and in your heart enable yourself to abhor the bad.

Enjoy reading books and true stories, hearing sermons and virtuous conversations. And if for committing a mortal sin, you win the world but lose your soul, do not pay such a high price.

Jack Benny

Music as a Bond Between Parent and Child

Growing up in Hollywood in the 1930s and 1940s, Joan Benny felt close to her famous actor-comedian father, but often wished for more direct guidance. "Perhaps I had seen too many Andy Hardy movies," Joan later recalled in *Sunday Nights at Seven: The Jack Benny Story*, "because he couldn't deal with my personal problems. Happily, during my late teen years, our relationship blossomed due to our mutual love of music."

From her earliest years, Joan loved to listen to records in her room and to sing and dance to the music. She soon "graduated" from the sound tracks of movies like *Snow White* and *The Wizard of Oz* to Beethoven, Tchaikovsky, and other classical composers. She recalled, "By the time I reached my teens, I had amassed a rather large collection of 78 RPM records." Among her favorite musical pieces was Handel's *Messiah*, which her parents had given her as a present on her thirteenth birthday. "[After] Daddy took up the violin again, a few years later, my knowledge and love of classical music would become the strongest bond between us."

Decades later, Joan reminisced, "When he began taking an interest in classical music, I could hardly believe my luck. It was a godsend. Now, not only could I share my musical passion, but the problem of what to buy Daddy for his birthday and Christmas was solved. No more boring ties and shirts, of which he already had closetsful. I gave him scores of violin concertos, recordings of violin concertos and, later, when I could afford it, two extra-special gifts—first editions of the Hill and Sons books on Stradivari and Guarneri. I even managed to get Jascha Heifitz to autograph the Stradivari one for him. Daddy was ecstatic, I triumphant!

"By now Daddy had an up-to-date stereo system in his bedroom. We spent many an hour listening to, comparing, and discussing different violinists playing the same piece. Heifitz, Stern, Francescatti, Milstein, Oistrakh—it was interesting and instructive to listen to each of them play the same selection. They became his heroes.

"Now that he was concertizing and had the opportunity to meet these artists, he was as excited as a little boy meeting Superman. And he found it hard to believe that a great concert performer could be impressed to meet him. A close friend of mine, musician Artie Kane, remembers: 'Once I made him angry. It was after a Rudolf Serkin concert, and Jack was telling us he'd been overwhelmed by his piano playing and had gone backstage to the green room. He couldn't get over it because Serkin ran to find a piece of paper so he could get Jack's autograph. I had just enough of his humility and said, "Jack, did it ever occur to you that he was twice as thrilled to meet you as you were to meet him?" He didn't like what I said. I didn't know why I'd made him angry because I was trying to compliment him. I realized later that he was right—he wanted to be impressed and I was spoiling it for him.'"

Joan Benny added, "Daddy and I read scores together as we listened, discussing the notation. I introduced him to chamber music. I remember he particularly loved the César Franck violin sonata and the Anton Dvořák *Dumky* trio. Daddy was fascinated with this new world he had discovered—and so proud of his 'brilliant' daughter. . . . He bragged about me to all his friends."

Samuel Bernstein and his son Leonard

———

A Father's Song

On a wintry Sunday in 1962, Samuel Bernstein celebrated his seventieth birthday at a lavish banquet in Boston. He was honored as a successful businessman with a philanthropic bent—not as composer Leonard Bernstein's father. Eight hundred prominent citizens attended, including the mayor of Boston, the lieutenant governor, and the attorney general of Massachusetts. When his turn came to speak, Leonard Bernstein spoke with great seriousness about the relationship between fathers and sons. At the time, he was grappling with a new composition, his *Kaddish* symphony, in which a narrator, the Speaker, conducts a defiant, somewhat violent debate with God. Bernstein did not complete the symphony until nearly eighteen months later, but its theme was clearly on his mind that celebratory night. He said:

> What is a father in the eyes of a child? The child feels: My father is first of all my authority, with power to dispense approval

or punishment. He is secondly my protector; thirdly my provider; beyond that he is healer, comforter, law-giver, because he caused me to exist. . . . And as the child grows up, he retains all his life, in some deep, deep part of him, the stamp of that father-image whenever he thinks of God, of good and evil, of retribution.

For example, take the idea of defiance. Every son, at one point or another, defies his father, fights him, departs from him, only to return to him—if he is lucky—closer and more secure than before. Again we see clearly the parallel with God: Moses protesting to God, arguing, fighting to change God's mind. So the child defies the father, and something of that defiance also remains throughout his life.

This was somber rhetoric for a birthday party, and Bernstein was sensible enough to lighten the mood in his conclusion. He acknowledged that since becoming a father himself nine years before, he had gained a better understanding of "the complex phenomenon that is Samuel J. Bernstein, for he is a great and multifaceted man."

Finally, the world-renowned composer took his audience back thirty years to what he recalled as his first public performance as a pianist, at Temple Mishkan Tefila near Boston. "I was playing a composition of my own. It was a series of variations on a tune my father was singing in the shower, and from hearing it sung so often I had gotten to be rather fond of it myself."

Then, in honor of his father's seventieth birthday, Leonard Bernstein announced that he had composed a new variation in his own style. He playfully called it "Meditation on a Prayerful Theme My Father Sang in the Shower Thirty Years Ago." He later incorporated it into his *Kaddish* symphony.

Kenko

Overcoming Lust

Kenko, one of Japan's great poets, served in the fourteenth-century imperial court. He became a Buddhist monk after the emperor's death. Kenko never fully withdrew from everyday life, but retired to a city temple in Kyoto, not far from the royal court whose elite interests and manners continued to fascinate him.

In his writings, Kenko celebrated Japanese traditions. He had refined, pronounced tastes, and venerated the past, although he preached about the impermanence of earthly existence. Toward the end of his life, Kenko, then a monk, wrote *Essays in Idleness*, advice to the young about the path to wisdom:

> Nothing leads a man astray as easily as sexual desire. What a foolish thing a man's heart is! Though we realize, for example, that fragrances are short-lived and the scent burnt into clothes lingers but briefly, how our hearts always leap when we catch a

whiff of an exquisite perfume! The holy man of Kume lost his magic powers after noticing the whiteness of the legs of a girl who was washing clothes. This was quite understandable, considering that the glowing plumpness of her arms, legs, and flesh owed nothing to artifice.

Leo Tolstoy

—

The Pursuit of Pleasure

After settling down to marriage and family life, Leo Tolstoy began his most productive literary period, producing such masterpieces as *War and Peace* and *Anna Karenina*. In middle age, Tolstoy devoted himself more to philosophical and social concerns, although he finally returned to writing.

In October 1895, Tolstoy sent this sternly moralistic letter about love to his sixteen-year-old son, Mikhail Lvovich:

> What you are probably dreaming about vaguely, without forming a clear picture of how it will come about—namely, that you will marry the object of your love and live a good life—is as improbable as winning with one ticket in a million. The need to get married is only legitimate in a man who is fully mature, and then meeting with a woman may cause you to fall in love. At your age, this is just simply over-indulgence, caused by your

luxurious, idle, and unprincipled life, and by the wish to imitate. Therefore what is most important, what is necessary for you now, is for you to come to your senses, to take a look at yourself and at the lives of other people, and ask yourself: What are you living for? And what do you want of yourself? . . . Pleasure comes as a reward only to the man who doesn't seek it or make it the goal of his life.

Samuel Taylor Coleridge

———

Overcoming Personal Faults

A philosopher-poet of the nineteenth-century English romantic movement, Coleridge wrote such enduring works as "The Rime of the
Ancient Mariner" and "Kubla Khan." Although Coleridge taught a
mystical outlook on life, in this letter, written in February 1807 to his
fourteen-year-old son Hartley, he offered no blissful visions, just practical advice:

> You are now going with me into Devonshire to visit your
> uncle. He is a very good man, and very kind, but his notions of
> right and of propriety are very strict. He is therefore exceedingly
> shocked by any gross deviations from what is proper. I take there-
> fore this means of warning you against those bad habits, which I
> and all of your friends here have noticed in you. Be assured, I
> am not writing in anger, but on the contrary, with great love.

First then, I conjure you never to do anything of any kind when out of sight which you would not do in my presence. What is a frail and faulty father on earth compared with God, your heavenly father? But God is always present.

When you have done wrong, acknowledge it at once, like a man. Excuses may show your ingenuity, but they make your honesty suspect. And a grain of honesty is better than a pound of wit. We may admire a man for his cleverness, but we love and esteem him only for his goodness. A strict attachment to truth, and to the whole truth, with openness and frankness and simplicity, is at once the foundation stone of all goodness and no small part of the superstructure. Lastly, do what you have to do at once—and put it out of hand. No procrastination, no self-delusion.

Take a little trouble with yourself, and everyone will be delighted and try to gratify you in all your reasonable wishes. Above all, you will be at peace with yourself—a double blessing.

Aldous Huxley

Maturity and Self-Awareness

Aldous Huxley emigrated from England in the late 1930s to become a highly paid Hollywood scriptwriter. With an iconoclastic streak, Huxley, whose novels included *Brave New World,* was also interested in mysticism, psychology, and the creative process, and wrote several books on these intriguing topics.

But Huxley's son Matthew, in his early twenties, was restlessly struggling to find his own niche in Southern California. In September 1943, his famous father offered this straight-from-the-shoulder advice:

> You are extremely critical of other people's shortcomings in the manner of self-indulgence and inconsiderateness and slackness—critical often to the point of intolerance. But you are *not* critical, you are all too tolerant, of the same shortcomings in yourself. Letting things slide, forgetting what ought to be remembered, not bothering to do things because you don't happen to

feel like doing them, permitting an immediate distraction, such as the purposeless reading of a magazine article, to get in the way of doing a present duty or thinking rationally about the future— these are things about which, in yourself, you are altogether too indulgent. For I think you permit yourself many things at home which you would not dream of doing when with other people.

Of course, this quirk is not confined to you alone. Many young people tend to permit themselves worse manners and less considerate behavior at home than with other people. But it is a sign of adulthood to realize that even one's closest relations deserve as much thought and as many small, boring self-sacrifices as do strangers.... And this will be made easier for you if, as I hope, you have definite chores to do in a routine that has to be strictly observed.

Rocco Buscaglia and his son Leo

———

Overcoming Prejudice

As a bestselling American author of books on intimacy, Leo Buscaglia is perhaps best known for touting the benefits of "daily hugs" with family members, friends, neighbors, and coworkers. A professor of education at the University of Southern California, Buscaglia always emphasized to his students that children vitally need emotional—not just academic—nurturing while growing up.

The son of Italian immigrants, Buscaglia was raised in Southern California. His parents spoke little English, and what they did use was thickly accented. "We ate different, exotic foods; our conversations were more animated; our voices a bit louder; our gestures more generous," Buscaglia recalled in his celebratory memoir, *Papa, My Father.* "As I grew to adolescence . . . suddenly Mama and Papa, whom I had loved without question, became an embarrassment."

One day, Buscaglia was assaulted by a gang of boys at his junior high school. They taunted him with ethnic slurs and punched him. Humiliated and angry, he ran home crying and locked himself in the bathroom, finally opening the door when his father gently called. Young Leo sobbed uncontrollably. His father hugged him and said, "Now tell me what happened."

"I hate being Italian!" he confessed angrily. "I wish I could be *anything* else!" Years later, Buscaglia recalled in his memoir:

> Papa held me firmly, his voice now strong and threatening. "Never let me hear you say that again!" he said. "You should be proud to be what you are. Just think about it. America was discovered by and got its name from Italians. Italians make sweet music, sing gloriously, paint wonderful pictures, write great books, and build beautiful bridges. How can you not be proud to be an Italian? And you're extra lucky because you're an American, too."
>
> "But they don't know that," I objected. "I'd rather be like everyone else."
>
> "Well, you're not like everyone else. God never intended us to be the same. He made us all different so that we'd each be ourselves. Never be afraid of differences. Difference is good. Would you want to be like the boys who beat you up and called you names? Would you want to make others suffer and cry? Aren't

you glad you're different from them?" I remember that I thought it was a weak argument, but I remained silent.

"Well, would you?" he insisted. "Would you want to be like them? Like the people who hurt you?"

"No."

"Then wipe your tears and be proud of who you are. You can be sure that it won't be the last time you'll meet these people. They're everywhere. Feel sorry for them, but don't be afraid of them. We've got to be strong and always be proud of who we are and what we are. Then nobody can hurt us."

He dried my tears and washed my face. "Now," he said, "let's get some bread and butter and go eat in the garden."

"Though I didn't find Papa's explanation very satisfying," Buscaglia observed later, "it somehow made me feel better. . . . Of course, Papa didn't solve the problems of bigotry on that sunny California day when we ate bread and butter in the garden. But there was something in his explanation, a certain strength and determination, that has continued to help me to see intolerance and discrimination for what they are: a refuge for weakness and ignorance."

Martin Luther King Jr.

———

Unpleasant Reality

In the early 1960s, the Reverend Martin Luther King Jr. found himself increasingly involved in the civil rights movement. In his rare free moments he devoted himself to his two young children, Yoki and Marty, at their home in Atlanta.

He played with both youngsters, trying to cram days and weeks into a few hours. His wife, Coretta, later recalled that he teased, tickled, and roughhoused with them until they nearly dismantled the house. Marty remembered that his father told them jokes, too, and was "really funny."

As parents, Martin and Coretta tried to mix discipline with understanding, because they realized that much of their children's adult character would be formed during their early years. Trying to learn from his own father's mistakes, King insisted that children need guidance—

not suppression—so they could learn to express their own ideas and feelings comfortably.

A friend once observed how relaxed King was with his children. As they talked in his study, Yoki and Marty would come in and ask him to settle an argument, which he would do. "You know," King once said to a visitor, "we adults are always so busy, we have so many things on our minds, we're so preoccupied, that we don't listen to our children. We say to them, 'See, Daddy's busy.' We tend to forget that they are trying to survive in a world they have to create for themselves. We forget how much creativity and resourcefulness that takes."

As his own father had done, King tried to shield his children from racial prejudice. But, inevitably, they had to experience that first upsetting awareness of what it meant to be "colored" in Dixie. For Yoki, it came when she pleaded with her father to take her to Funtown, a segregated amusement park in Atlanta. Initially King gave her an evasive answer, but then one day, she ran downstairs full of excitement.

Yoki had just seen a television commercial inviting everyone to visit Funtown and couldn't wait to go, After hearing that, Yoki's parents sat down with her and for the first time tried to explain about segregation. "I have won some applause as a speaker," King later observed, "but my tongue twisted and my speech stammered seeking to explain to my six-year-old daughter why the public invitation on television didn't include her and others like her. One of the most painful experiences

I have ever faced was to see her tears when I told her that Funtown was *closed* to colored children . . . for at that moment the first dark cloud . . . had floated into her little mental sky."

In the ensuing years on the lecture circuit, when King spoke about the injuries of racial prejudice, he would often recount his troubling conversation with Yoki about Funtown. He would set an example for Yoki and all children by fighting for freedom now.

William Dean Howells

———

Parting

William Dean Howells was one of the most widely read American writers of the late nineteenth century. He was known for his literary realism in works like *The Rise of Silas Lapham*. As an editor, biographer, novelist, and critic, Howells had a major impact upon American culture, including helping to launch the careers of writers like Mark Twain.

In September 1896, Howells sent this encouraging letter to his twenty-one-year-old son John, who had been conflicted and indecisive about leaving home to finish studying art in Paris:

> It seems very strange to have you gone. I lived very intensely in your presence, and I won't deny that I hated to have you go. I can now understand my own father's feelings in his partings with me, and when you have a son, you will repeat our sad experience. But this is life, and I accept our separation as part of the

common lot. You have gone about your duty, and that is enough. I was sorry and ashamed to be overcome a little at the last; at the very last, when I stood grinning at you from the wharf, I was really gay.

I hope you will find your work waiting for you in the right shape, and your mind and hand grown in cunning as they do in an interval of desistance. I think I shall be better able to appreciate your work hereafter, and you know how glad I shall be to know all you can tell me about it.

Andrea Cuomo and his son Mario

Perseverance

As New York State's governor for twelve years, Mario Cuomo often referred to his working-class origins with pride and eloquence. His father, Andrea, and mother, Immaculata, were Neopolitan immigrants who came to the United States in the late 1920s.

Lacking formal schooling, Andrea Cuomo cleaned sewers for several years before saving enough money to open a grocery store located in a multiethnic New York City neighborhood. "It was open twenty-four hours a day, and by the time I was born in 1932," his famous son later recalled, "my father was making a living from sandwiches he made in the early morning for the construction crews and quick midnight snacks he prepared for the night shift in the factory across the street. . . . Almost everything he did, he did for his children."

In 1982, Mario Cuomo first ran successfully for New York State's governorship. Exhausted and sleepless one night just before the

"FATHER, IT'S RAINING."   "OH, WELL, LET IT RAIN."   "I WAS GOING TO, FATHER."

election, he became inspired in remembering his father. Two years later, *The Diaries of Mario Cuomo* provided his account:

> I was looking for a pencil, rummaging through some papers in the back of my desk drawer, when I turned up one of Papa's old business cards, the ones we made up for him, that he was so proud of: *ANDREA CUOMO, ITALIAN-AMERICAN GROCERIES—FINE IMPORTED PRODUCTS.* Papa never had any occasion to give anyone a calling card, but he loved having them. He put one in a little gold frame on a red velvet background on the nightstand near his bed. Momma has one of them now, framed Like Papa's, on display in a prominent place in her in china closet.
>
> I couldn't help wondering what Papa would have said if I told him that I was tired—or God forbid—that I was discouraged. Then I thought for a few minutes about how he dealt with hard circumstances. A thousand different pictures flashed through my mind—he was so used to dealing with hard circumstances. Almost everything was hard.
>
> But one scene in particular came sharply into view.
>
> We had just moved into Holliswood from behind the store. We had our own house for the first time; it even had some land around it, even trees—one, in particular, was a great blue spruce that must have been forty feet high.

"Holliswood was hilly. Our house sat ten or fifteen feet above the road itself, and the blue spruce stood majestically like a sentinel at the corner of our property, where the street made a turn, bending around our property line.

Less than a week after we moved in there was a terrible storm. We came home from the store that night to find the great blue spruce pulled almost totally out of the ground and flung forward, its mighty nose bent in the asphalt of the street. Frankie and I knew nothing about trees. We could climb poles all day; we were great at fire escapes; we could scale fences with barbed wire at the top—but we knew nothing about trees. When we saw our spruce, defeated, its cheek on the canvas, our hearts sank. But not Papa's.

Maybe he was five feet six if his heels were not worn. Maybe he weighed one hundred and fifty-five pounds if he had had a good meal. Maybe he could see a block away if his glasses were clean. But he was stronger than Frankie and I and Marie and Momma all together.

We stood in the street looking down at the tree. The rain was falling. We waited a couple of minutes, figuring things out, and then he announced, "O.K., we gonna push 'im up!" "What are you talking about, Papa? The roots are out of the ground!"

"Shut up, we gonna push 'im up, he's gonna grow again."

We didn't know what to say to him, you couldn't say no to

him; not just because you were his son, but because he was so sure.

So we followed him into the house and got what rope there was and we tied the rope around the tip of the tree that lay in the asphalt, and he stood up by the house, with me pulling on the rope and Frankie in the street in the rain, helping to push up the great blue spruce. In no time at all we had it standing up straight again!

With the rain still falling, Papa dug away at the place where the roots were, making a muddy hole wider and wider as the tree sank lower and lower toward security. Then we shoveled mud over the roots and moved boulders to the base of the tree to keep it in place. Papa drove stakes in the ground, tied rope from the trunk to the stakes, and maybe two hours later looked at the spruce, the crippled spruce made straight by ropes, and said, "Don't worry, he's gonna grow again."

I looked at the card and wanted to cry. If you were to drive past the house today you would see the great, straight blue spruce, maybe sixty-five feet tall, pointing straight up to the heavens, pretending it never had its nose in the asphalt.

I put Papa's card back in the drawer, closed it with a vengeance. I couldn't wait to get back into the campaign.

Thomas Edison

Effort

Celebrated as the Wizard of Menlo Park, self-taught Thomas Edison was a quintessential inventor-entrepreneur who, through most of his career, devoted little time to his own family. However, after achieving international adulation, he enjoyed offering paternal advice to young scientists beginning their careers. In January 1909, when Edison was fifty-six years old, a new research employee naively said, "Please tell me what laboratory rules you want me to observe." This was Edison's forceful reply:

> Hell! There ain't no rules around here! We are trying to accomplish something. . . . Do you believe in luck? For my part, I do not believe in luck at all—good or bad. Most fellows try a few things and then quit. *I* never quit until I get what I'm after. That's the only difference between me, that's supposed to be lucky, and the fellows that think they are unlucky.

Then again, a lot of people think that I have done things because of some "genius" that I've got. That too is not true. Any other bright-minded fellow can accomplish just as much if he will stick like hell and remember that nothing that's any good works by itself, just to please you; you have to *make* the damn thing work. You may have heard people repeat what I have said, "Genius is one percent inspiration, 99 percent perspiration." Yes, sir, it's mostly *hard work*.

Harry Truman

A Good Name

Harry Truman's presidency was marked by such momentous events as the dropping of the atomic bomb on Japan, the Allied victory in World War II, the start of the Cold War, and the Korean War. During the decades since Truman's administration ended in 1952, historians have come to regard him with increasing respect. As a father, Truman was extremely close to his only child, Margaret, who was born in 1924.

Writing to Margaret in February 1947, he had a direct, intimate style in counseling her about her ambition to become a professional singer:

> I hope your work is getting results. It takes work, work, and more work to get satisfactory results, as your pop can testify. Don't go off the deep end on contracts until you know for sure what you are getting—and what you have to offer.

I am only interested in your welfare and happy future, and I stand ready to do anything to contribute to that end. But remember that good name and honor are worth more than all the gold and jewels ever mined. Remember what old man Shakespeare said, "Who steals my purse steals trash, but who filches my good name takes that which enriches not himself and makes me poor indeed." A good name and good advice is all your old dad can give you.

Charlie Chaplin

———

Planning an Acting Career

Charlie Chaplin's marriage to his second wife, actress Lita Grey, ended in bitter divorce in 1927. At the time, the six-hundred-thousand-dollar settlement, with a trust fund for each of their babies—Charlie Jr. and Sydney—was the largest in American legal history. For the next few years, Chaplin had little contact with his young sons. Then, in the summer of 1932, Lita arranged for them to debut as actors by appearing with her in a new movie entitled *The Little Teacher*.

Returning from France to New York, the children were met by a battery of photographers and reporters. Seven-year-old Charlie Jr. modestly announced that he was going to be a great actor and would like to play cowboys. Six-year-old Sydney confided that he was going to be Mickey Mouse.

Chaplin was furious and immediately filed a legal petition objecting to the boys working in motion pictures. At the subsequent hearing, the judge ruled in his favor. Charlie Jr. and Sydney cried with disappointment upon hearing the news, and their father offered a serious response:

> If you're really in earnest about wanting to act, going into it now would be the worst thing in the world for you boys. You'd be typed as child actors. When you reached the gawky stage, they'd drop you. Then you would have to make a complete comeback and you'd have a hard time of it, because everyone would remember you as those cute little juveniles. But if after you've grown up you still want to act, then I won't interfere.

In later years, the two boys came to appreciate their father's advice. But at the time, they were less convinced, partly, no doubt, because their playmates included the renowned child star Shirley Temple.

Isaac Asimov

Playfulness and Humor in Parenting

"I must admit that although I don't like children," America's famous science-fiction writer once revealed, "I find little girls far more tolerable than little boys." After the birth of their son, David, when his wife was thirty-five years old and had already experienced fertility problems, Isaac Asimov expected no more children, But less than four years later their daughter, Robyn, was born.

"Robyn didn't cry much," reminisced Asimov in his third autobiography, published shortly before his death. "She was good natured; she toilet-trained quickly; and in all ways she was satisfactory, except that she did have the habit of (once in a while) drinking her formula and then quietly giving it back to me all over my shirt.

"Most of all, she grew into a beautiful, blond-haired, blue-eyed child. At seven, she looked precisely like the John Tenniel illustrations of Alice in *Alice in Wonderland*. This was so marked that when she walked into a new class at school, the teacher took one look at her and asked her to play Alice in the school play.

THE EXCURSION.

Head of Family. "I RECKON SOME OF US 'LL HAVE TO STAND, OR WE SHAN'T ALL GET SEATS!"

"I was delighted and could never hug and kiss her enough and tell her how beautiful she was. [My wife] Gertude objected (thinking perhaps of her own childhood) and said I shouldn't do that. 'What if she grows up to be a plain woman?' she said.

"I said stoutly, 'She won't. And even if she does, she'll be beautiful in my eyes, and I want her always to know that.'

"And, as it happened, she grew up to be extraordinarily beautiful in anyone's eyes. She is five feet two inches tall, her mother's height, still has blond hair, though her eyes have darkened. More important than beautiful, she is a sweet girl, softhearted and loving, who returns her father's affection in full."

One day when Robyn was a young adult, Asimov was chatting with a family visitor and mentioned Robyn's warm affection for him. Perhaps a bit cynically, the visitor replied, " Look, if you had a well-off father who dotes on you, what's not to like?"

His feelings hurt by the remark's implications, Asimov decided that his daughter would be able to give him a truthful answer. He therefore said to her, "Robyn, would you love me if I were poor?"

She answered without hesitation. "Of course, you'd still be crazy, wouldn't you?"

Asimov later wrote, "And that satisfied me. It was clear that she valued spending her life laughing and considered that more important than any money I might have."

John F. Kennedy

—

Playing on the Team

John F. Kennedy was very much enamored of his two children, Caroline and John Jr. In January 1961, when the forty-three-year-old Kennedy took office as president, his daughter was a toddler and his son newly born. Later, President Theodore Roosevelt's daughter Alice Roosevelt Longworth was visiting the Kennedys at the White House and observed how casually the children ran around the family's living quarters on the second floor. She remarked, "This is just the way it was when I lived here."

Caroline made it a ritual to walk with her father downstairs to work every morning. She called him Silly Daddy and he called her Buttons. She had a way of parking herself on his lap during breakfast meetings with the presidential staff. He always let her stay. Or Caroline might walk imperiously into a meeting to announce in a loud and clear voice, "Mommy wants you!"

Jackie later said of her husband, "Most men don't care about children as much as women do, but he did. He was the kind of man who should have had a brood of children."

During the presidential campaign, he had hardly seen Caroline, but once in the White House, Kennedy reveled in her personality and accomplishments. He taught Caroline short poems, which she memorized, and invented tales for her. Before she was three years old, Caroline drew a birthday card for him. When she once skinned her knee and was about to cry, he said gently, "Kennedys don't cry."

Cynical observers remarked that the Kennedy children were part of the political act, and it is true that photographers were often around when Caroline and John Jr. came into the Oval Office to call on their father, crawl onto his lap, or hide under his desk. It made for good publicity. But the photographers weren't there every morning when Kennedy would say to little John, "Come on, let's get to work." And dressed in his pajamas, the toddler would walk with his father to the Oval Office. For a while, there was even a rocking horse in the Cabinet Room. The president told the Cabinet that, "we keep that rocking horse in here to remind us of the younger generation and what our responsibilities are [to them]."

Upon the birth of a new nephew, Kennedy addressed this humorous letter to him:

"Welcome, to the youngest member of the clan. Your entrance is timely, as we need a new left end on the team. Here's hoping you do not acquire the political assets of your parents, the prolific qualities of your godfather [Bobby], or the problems of your uncle."

On one occasion, Joseph Kennedy teasingly said to his son, the president, "Caroline's very bright, smarter than you were at that age."

"Yes, she is," was the instant quip, "but look who *she has* for a father!"

Ralph Waldo Emerson

━━━

Praising Grown-up Children

A revered figure in nineteenth-century American philosophy, Ralph Waldo Emerson inspired numerous writers and thinkers including his close friend Henry David Thoreau, Emily Dickinson, Herman Melville, and Henry James. Originally a Unitarian minister, in the 1830s Emerson became immensely successful as an independent writer and lecturer. His key themes included self-reliance, individuality, and reverence for nature.

Emerson was a doting father to his four children, especially to his younger daughter, Edith, born in 1841. At the age of twenty-four, she married William Forbes, the son of a wealthy Boston merchant, and settled nearby in the town of Milton. Dismayed that their previously close relationship seemed to be weakening, Emerson offered this outlook in April 1867:

I mean now to find a way of coming to your house at short periods and *so* keeping my children around me. As we drive it, it is rarely and casually that friends meet who have yet a high esteem for each other. In the same house or in the same room, one or both may be so diverted by their own work, or by other persons, that they two do not once fairly converse. Well, we acquiesce in this as instinctive and best for both, provided we can only now and then secure one full radiant gaze, or a pair of cordial words.

It is plain that in general we are ever on the hunt for comparative strangers, but later we discover that we may find some of our best friends in our own blood. You are a very good girl and have been nobly true, and all the more because so quiet, to your own convictions. I like so to say this because it is the glory of character to be thus, without hearing of it, or expecting to hear, and yet the observer wants to say: Thanks and persist.

John D. Rockefeller Sr.

———

Slow and Sturdy

John D. Rockefeller Sr. emerged from a farming background to became one of the richest people in the world. He started working full-time when he was sixteen years old, and within a few years, had already opened his first successful business in Cleveland. Rockefeller had the reputation of being stern and penny-pinching with his children.

Upon graduating from Brown University in 1897, his only son, John D. Rockefeller Jr.—known as Junior—began working in his father's office on lower Broadway, the headquarters of Standard Oil in New York City. At the age of twenty-three, he was given no instructions about his duties but was expected to assume responsibilities as they arose. At the outset, Junior was made assistant to his father's chief aide, for Rockefeller Sr. had already begun semiretirement.

In the summer of 1899, Junior took an extended recreational trip to the Far West and Alaska with friends. By this point in his life, he must have deeply impressed Rockefeller Sr., who wrote him this letter of encouragement:

I have your beautiful letter of the seventh. We are so glad that you feel better for the vacation and we all hope you will hold the ground gained and be sure to take more rest, and change whenever you think you will need it. We all join in thanking you over and over again, for as we review the journey, we are led to appreciate more than we could have expressed to you the plan you adopted and executed in such a thoroughly satisfactory way.

We receive our pay from you as we go, ten fold. Confidence is a plant of slow growth, but in your case, it was a sturdy plant long years ago. We are grateful beyond measure that we can trust, and do trust you in every place without reserve.

Be sure to take good care of your health. This is the first consideration.

Douglas MacArthur

—————

Pride in Being a Father

Though General Douglas MacArthur was notorious as a tough, humorless military commander, he exhibited a complete personality change when it came to Arthur, his only son. Arthur was born in the Philippines in 1938, when tensions between Japan and the United States were steadily mounting in the Pacific. His well-known father was already almost sixty years old.

When Arthur began to walk, and then to talk, father and son created a morning ceremony. Each day at about 7:30 A.M., the general's bedroom door would open and the lad would trudge in clutching his favorite toy, a stuffed rabbit with a scraggly mustache which he called Old Friend.

MacArthur would immediately jump out of bed and snap to attention. Then, the general would march around the room in quickstep as his son counted cadence: "Boom! Boom! Boomity boom!" After they had passed the bed several times, Arthur would cover his eyes with his hands, while his father produced that day's particular present: a piece of candy, a crayon, or a coloring book. The ceremony would end in the bathroom, where MacArthur would shave while Arthur watched, and they sang duets: "Sweet Rosie O'Grady," "Roamin' in the Gloamin'"— burring all the *r*'s—or "Army Blue."

Some two weeks after the Japanese bombing of Pearl Harbor on December 7, the MacArthur family joined the mass evacuation of Manila. The general's wife, Jean, had already decorated a Christmas tree for their son Arthur and had filled a closet with presents, including a new tricycle, for him. It seemed clear that they would be elsewhere on December 25.

Not wishing to spoil the holiday for Arthur, the family pretended that it was already Christmas. Elated, their son played with his new toys as though nothing were amiss. As they had predicted, only hours before Christmas Eve actually arrived, all United States military personnel, including the MacArthurs, had to flee before the city's impending fall.

While leading the Allies' Pacific offensive in 1943, MacArthur won an award in the United States as Father of the Year. Profoundly moved by this honor, he sent the following cable:

> Nothing has touched me more deeply than the act of the National Father's Day Committee. By profession I am a soldier

and take great pride in that fact, but I am also prouder, infinitely prouder, to be a father. A soldier destroys in order to build; the father only builds, never destroys. The one has the potentialities of death; the other embodies creation and life. And while the hordes of death are mighty, the battalions of life are mightier still. It is my hope that my son when I am gone will remember me, not from the battle, but in the home, repeating with him our simple daily prayer, "Our Father Who Art in Heaven."

Nicholas Earp and his son Wyatt

———

Respect for the Law

Born in Western Illinois in 1848, Wyatt Earp became famous as America's greatest gunfighting marshal. Branded a hero and a killer for bringing law and order to frontier outposts like Wichita and Dodge City, Kansas, and Tombstone, Arizona, he embodied the Old West for millions—and his life became the stuff of legends. Yet, unknown to most, Earp enjoyed a peaceful Los Angeles retirement until 1929, when death quietly took him at the age of eighty.

The famous gunslinger was childless, but always had fond memories of his father, Nicholas Earp, a successful, wealthy, and much-admired frontier farmer. Shortly before Wyatt's death, he reminisced for a biographer:

> Father's regard for the land was equaled by his respect for the law and his detestation for the lawless element so prevalent in the West. I heard him say many times that, while the law might

not be entirely just, it generally expressed the will of the decent folks who were trying to build up the country, and that until someone could offer a better safeguard for [one's] rights, enforcement of the law was the duty of [all] who asked for its protection in any way.

Nicholas Earp also held strong convictions about the value of education. His children took what the village schools could offer and were required to follow more advanced studies at home. Until Wyatt was sixteen years old and opted for frontier adventure, he was regarded as the family's successor to his grandfather's legal practice and was coached for this career.

Marshal Earp recalled,

As we grew older, we were given to understand that it was our conduct toward others which really counted . . . and [we] were thoroughly grounded in this practical creed, and left to our own devices as far as religion was concerned. "Religion," my father once observed to me, "is a matter which every [person] must settle for himself."

Herman Melville

———

Respect for Your Mother

Born in New York City, Herman Melville served with the United States Navy and went to sea on several whaling ships before settling down to a literary career. He gained great popularity for such works as *Typee* (1846), *Omoo* (1847), and *Redburn* (1849). Ironically, Melville's most enduring novel, *Moby-Dick* (1851), was poorly received by readers and critics alike during his own lifetime.

In September 1860, when the forty-one-year-old Melville was on a ship in the Pacific Ocean, heading home to the New York area, he offered these words about motherhood to his eight-year-old son Malcolm:

> I hope that you have called to mind what I said to you about your behavior previous to my going away. I hope that you have been obedient to your mother and helped her all you could and

A NATURAL INFERENCE.

"Oh, Mamma, I know what you mean by *sound* asleep now. Just listen to Papa!"

saved her trouble. Now is the time to show what you are—whether you are a good, honorable boy, or a good-for-nothing one.

Any boy of your age who disobeys his mother, or worries her, or is disrespectful to her—such a boy is a poor, shabby fellow; and, if you know any such boys, you ought to cut their acquaintance.

Moshe Zelig Hakohen

———

Rules to Live By

During the early-to-mid-nineteenth century, Moshe Zelig Hakohen served as Latvia's leading rabbi. The Jewish community actively sought his guidance on ritual, social conduct, family matters, and many different legal questions. In January 1849, the esteemed rabbi wrote an "ethical will," in keeping with a longstanding tradition in Judaism. This will contained more than sixty-five specific recommendations for his children and grandchildren on how to lead an upright life. These included:

1. Strengthen oneself to arise in the morning to the service of the Creator.
2. Cleanse the body thoroughly.
3. Pray with utmost devotion.
4. Control oneself.

5. Be long-suffering. Be among the insulted, never the insulters; among those who are insulted but never respond in kind, even when it is by a household member.

6. If possible, eat to somewhat less than full satiety.

7. Avoid vows and oaths and all things doubtful.

8. Beware of deceit.

9. Avoid any sharp business transactions and whatever is contrary to the law and honesty.

10. Write down all items and subjects that require improvement in matters of personal traits or good deeds, each according to the requirement.

11. Never walk haughtily.

12. Write down any and all miraculous and wondrous occurrences that happen to you.

13. Avoid a business transaction that appears difficult to complete successfully.

14. Remove yourself from anger and pride to the utmost extent.

15. Trust in God, that He will certainly do everything for your benefit—for "What is past is no more, and the future's still in store."

Seneca

Building Character

Born in Spain, the first-century Roman writer and orator Seneca the Younger espoused a stoic philosophy about life. His father was an accomplished rhetorician and writer in his own right. The emperor Claudius eventually exiled Seneca—who had become very popular—for advocating social equality, reason, and simple living. During this period of persecution, Seneca wrote various "moral letters" to a younger civil servant named Lucilius. Regarded as the foundation for the modern essay, these pieces offered advice about building character:

> When they are in the open, vices invariably take a more moderate form; diseases too are on the way toward being cured once they have broken out, instead of being latent, and made their presence felt. So it is with the love of money, the love of power, and the other maladies that affect the minds of men—you may be

sure that it is when they abate and give every appearance of being cured that they are at their most dangerous.

We give the impression of being in retirement, and are nothing of the kind. For if we are genuine in this, if we have sounded the retreat and really turned away from the surface show, then nothing will distract us. Men and birds together in full chorus will never break into our thinking when that thinking is good and has at last come to be of a sure and steady character.

Thomas Watson Sr.

Assets and Liabilities

During his forty-two years as IBM's chief executive, Thomas Watson Sr. was one of America's most powerful and wealthy businessmen. He was also a concerned father of four children and eventually passed on IBM's leadership to his older son, Thomas Jr.

Growing up in Short Hills, New Jersey, in the 1920s, Thomas Jr. had both learning and behavior problems. Even arrested once for vandalism, he became known as Terrible Thomas Watson. As a young adult, Thomas Jr. was more disciplined, but found academics at Brown University difficult and frustrating. He felt ready to give up completely. In response, Thomas Sr. began an active correspondence, offering this intriguing advice in December 1936:

> Always remember life is not as complex as many people would have you think. And the older you grow, the more you will real-

ize that success and happiness depend on a very few things. I list the important assets and liabilities as follows:

Liabilities	Assets
Reactionary ideas!	Vision
Love of money!	Unselfishness
Unwholesome companions!	Love
Lax character!	Character (Good)
Lack of love for others!	Good manners
False friends	Friendship (Real)
	Pride in Record

As Thomas Jr. later recalled, "I had always disliked hearing such stuff, but now it seemed pretty well intentioned." Indeed, he soon completed Brown, and then, as his father's apprentice, successfully rose to the top of IBM.

Theodore Roosevelt

—

Sports and Character

Theodore Roosevelt was a man who loved physical action. Growing up frail and sickly with asthma, he refused to accept medical advice to live a sedentary life. Instead, Roosevelt deliberately sought to strengthen himself by vigorous exercise and sports. As an admired Rough Rider and an influential political leader for a generation, he made the phrase "Speak softly and carry a big stick" famous and counseled his children to "Hit the line hard." Yet Roosevelt always valued character and intelligence more than physical prowess.

Writing from the White House in October 1903, President Roosevelt offered this lucid guidance to his sixteen-year-old son, Theodore Jr., who was beginning his studies at Harvard:

> I am delighted to have you play football. I believe in rough, manly sports. But I do not believe in them if they degenerate into the sole end of anyone's existence. I don't want you to sacrifice

standing well in your studies to any over-athleticism; and I need not tell you that character counts for a great deal more than either intellect or body in winning success in life. . . .

[One] must develop his physical prowess up to a certain point; but after he has reached that point, there are other things that count more. In my regiment, nine-tenths of the men were better horsemen than I was, and probably two-thirds of them better shots than I was, while on the average they were certainly hardier and more enduring. Yet, after I had them a very short while they all knew, and I knew too, that nobody else could command them as I could.

I am glad you should play football; I am glad that you should ride and shoot and walk and row as well as you do. I should be very sorry if you did not do these things. But don't ever get into the frame of mind which regards these things as constituting the end to which all your energies must be devoted.

Colin Powell

———

Taking Risks

Raised in the Bronx by immigrant parents from Jamaica, Colin
Powell's rise to become America's most prominent military figure has
been widely acclaimed in the press. But much less is known about him
as a father of three children. Speaking for his wife, Alma, and himself,
Powell in his autobiography *My American Journey* intriguingly com-
mented, "We rarely know what our [grown] children think of us,
what, from the flood of childhood impressions and memories, stands
out and what fades." Then he added:

> Where the children are concerned, I never believed that pos-
> sessions could buy love, popularity, respect, or accomplishment.
> Consequently, I have always been careful about giving them
> money. They received an allowance of two dollars a week when
> they reached the age of twelve. They wanted for nothing; but

they were taught not to want too much. And on the big holidays, Christmas and birthdays, they got the big presents.

When Mike reached his teens, I thought it was time to give him some grounding in the facts of life. The way I handled the matter was direct, but I am not sure how courageous. I stopped by his room one night and handed him a paper bag with a book in it entitled *Boys and Sex*. "What's this?" he asked. "Read it," I answered, "and let me know if you have any questions."

As each of my children reached age sixteen, I wrote him or her a letter trying to pass along what I hoped was wisdom, or at least the benefit of my right choices and mistakes; Mike was first, and I wrote, among other things:

"You now begin to leave childhood behind and start on the road to manhood. . . . You will establish definitively the type [of] person you will be the remaining fifty years of your lifetime. Temptations will come your way, drugs, alcohol, opportunities for misbehaving. You know what is right and wrong, and I have confidence in your judgment. . . . Don't be afraid of failure. Be more afraid of not trying. . . . Take chances and risks—not foolhardy actions, but actions which could result in failure, yet promise success and great reward. And always remember that no matter how bad something may seem, it will not be that bad tomorrow."

Yitzhak Rabin

―――

Teaching Self-Acceptance

Israel's martyr for peace, assassinated prime minister Yitzhak Rabin, had a public image of gruffness. Even his admirers readily admitted that Rabin did not exude personal warmth and lacked the talent for effectively making small talk. But when it came to his children and grandchildren, Rabin revealed a very different side.

As prime minister, Rabin was continuously absorbed in his work. But his grandson Yonatan told a television interviewer after the assassination, "He was also a grandfather. Everyone would say, 'How does he have time for you?' And it was unbelievable how the man didn't miss a a single ceremony of mine or my sister Noa's. Not one. Every school ceremony, every army ceremony. . . . He got to them all."

Rabin's daughter Delia recalled he did the same thing when she was young. "He didn't come to parent-teacher meetings in school, he wasn't part of that," Dalia told an interviewer. "But when a need arose,

Small Boy (to R.A., Chevalier of the Legion of Honour, etc., etc). "OH, FATHER, IF YOU DON'T MIND, I THINK WE'LL TURN BACK HERE. THERE ARE SOME OF OUR FELLOWS COMING ALONG AND—YOU'RE ALL *RIGHT*, YOU KNOW—BUT THEY DON'T LIKE YOUR TIE!"

most of all when we were sick, he was always with us. He'd be called wherever he was, and he'd come. . . . He'd drop in for a few minutes to see me. He was a very, very concerned father."

His widow, Leah Rabin, reminisced, "He'd never raise his voice, or his hand, to one of the children. He'd always be loving and never put pressure on the children because of what he expected from them. I think that's the way to give children the feeling they are loved in any situation, any time, even if they don't live up to all your expectations. That was Yitzhak's secret: The children never owed him anything."

Rabin's favorite piece of advice for Dalia and her younger brother Yuval is one they have always remembered and tried to heed:

> Be comfortable with yourselves. The moment you are comfortable with yourself, and confident that you are doing the right thing, you can go forward. And never mind what anyone says about you.

Lincoln Steffens

———

Teamwork

A crusading journalist, Lincoln Steffens became famous at the turn of the twentieth century as a muckraker seeking major reforms in American society. Exposing the greed, corruption, and sordid dealings of politicians and "captains of industry" in countless newspaper and magazine articles, Steffens helped arouse the nation's social conscience.

In a letter of November 1933, Steffens offered this vivid advice—on the importance of teamwork—to his young son Peter:

> You have had your ninth birthday, turned the critical age of nine. Do you feel the difference? You must. There are a lot of your kid tastes that you should pass. No more stealing, no more lying; better table and other manners. For you have to clear the deck for ten. You will, of course. I am not a bit worried.
>
> I went to the Harvard–Yale football game yesterday. Harvard won by 19–6, and rejoiced because for two or three years Yale

had always won. It was teamwork that did it, teamwork, discipline, and skill. . . . One fine play is described by the papers as a nine-yard run, but I saw it and the point I noted was that the Harvard team—the whole team, opened the way clear for their runner and blocked the Yale players so that all their runner had to do was run. See? It was the team, not the runner, that did it.

The papers, the crowds, like and praise the individual players, but football is great because it is the teams, not the individuals, who play it when it is well played. Each individual player has to be good, skillful, perfect, but perfect only as the part of a perfect machine, which is the ideal.

Bret Harte

The Importance of Schoolwork

Even earlier than Mark Twain, Bret Harte was the first literary figure of the American West. His poem, "The Heathen Chinese," and his stories, collected in *The Luck of Roaring Camp and Other Sketches* (1870), made Harte the most famous living American author of his time.

In January 1879, while traveling abroad in Germany, Harte was inspired to advise his sixteen-year-old son Griswold ("Wodie") about educational success:

> Papa wants his big boy to grow up as *strong* as he is *tall*, and, if Papa is to be obliged to "look up" to his eldest son, he wants to have something nice to look at.
>
> Now, my eldest boy, I want you to "pitch in" and study as hard as you can. I have not heard that you are *not* studying, but I tell you this because I know that, if you were here in Germany with

me, you would be a little ashamed to see how hard these German boys study, and how much they know. They all study English and French as a rule, and some speak both languages fluently. Yet they are not naturally *bright* boys. It's all *hard work* with them, but they keep at it conscientiously. They begin their studies as early as seven o'clock in winter and do not leave school until four o'clock, and study in the evening.

Everbody here has the greatest belief and admiration for American clever children, and I should not like them to find you backward, or not up to them in mere study. I only say this, Wodie dear, by way of caution to you ... and now Papa has done his preaching.

W. C. Fields

<hr>

The Value of Education

Born in Philadelphia, William Claude Fields began his entertainment career as a fourteen-year-old vaudeville and musical-comedy performer. His trademarks as an adult included a top hat, a bulbous nose, and a distinctive side-of-the-mouth manner of speaking.

In movies like *My Little Chickadee* and *Never Give a Sucker an Even Break,* Fields portrayed cynical characters who preferred alcohol and swindling to the company of children. But in this advice to his young son, Claude—which Fields wrote in April 1915 while performing abroad—he revealed a tender, encouraging side:

> I was proud to receive such a fine letter from you written on the 29th, *ultimo*. I am glad to know you are going on so fine with your baseball and your gym work. Plenty of outdoor, strenuous exercise along with your studies will make you a fine man. I note

what you say about Europe and agree with you. You will find teachers here that are just as good as [in the United States]. But if you went abroad, you would lose one of the greatest privileges this country gives, that is, an American education.

Evelyn Waugh

―――

Staying in School

One of England's most widely read novelists of the twentieth century, Evelyn Waugh is known for his satiric portrayals of wealthy London society. His most famous novel, *Brideshead Revisited,* was published in 1945. He combined a razor-sharp wit with a focus on moral, and later religious, themes about upper-class life.

In this letter dated February 1956, Waugh wrote to his rebellious sixteen-year-old son, Auberon, who wanted to quit boarding school to enter the hotel trade:

> I have much sympathy with your restlessness with school life. I felt as you do at your age, asked my father to remove me, was resentful when he refused. Now I am grateful to him.
>
> If there was anything you ardently wished to do—go to sea, learn a skilled trade, etc., because you felt a real vocation for it, I would not stand in your way. I believe you think of hotel-keeping

simply as a means of leaving school. That is a very poor motive for taking a job, and hotel-keeping is not a craft which fits you for anything else. . . . If you leave school now, you will not get a commission in a good regiment. Perhaps you will not get commissioned at all.

Most of the interests and amusement of life come from one's friends. All my friends are those I met at Oxford or in the army. You are condemning yourself either to a lonely manhood or one among second-rate associates. All because you lack the willpower and self-control to make a success of the next eighteen months by . . . throwing yourself into the life of the school, doing your work and obeying the rules. . . . You have a sense of humor and a good gift of self-expression. On the other hand, you are singularly imprudent and you have a defective sense of honor. These bad qualities can lead to disaster.

My financial interests have no bearing on my wish for your welfare. I am sorry you should suggest that they might.

Louis Koch and his son Edward

———

The Value of Hard Work

Best known for his "How'm I doing?" approach to politics and life, Ed Koch served as New York City's mayor for twelve tumultuous years. Since leaving public office in 1989, he has remained active as a popular radio talk-show host, newspaper columnist, and a highly placed Manhattan attorney.

Koch grew up in New York City and Newark in the 1920s and 30s. He liked to joke in later years that, he had "moved from one slum to another." His father, Louis Koch, was a Polish-Jewish immigrant who never learned to write English well. He had struggled as a young peddler before immigrating to the United States and eventually opening a furrier shop. The small business never thrived, and when the Depression began, it shut down permanently.

Though hardly a success by social standards, Louis was important as a father who, in his daily life, taught the traits of fortitude and effort. Decades later in *Citizen Koch,* Ed Koch recalled:

I was seven years old at the time of our move from the Bronx, and it seemed as if my world had been reinvented: a new sister, a new apartment, a new extended family living under the same roof, a new neighborhood. It must have seemed that way to my father, too. He was broke, out of the fur business, and forced to work for his brother-in-law. Uncle Louis owned a dance hall in Newark called Kruger's Auditorium, and he leased the hatcheck business to my parents. The concession never brought in what we needed to get by; sometimes my father worked a second job, usually as a day laborer for a Manhattan furrier. There were even periods when he worked at a third job.

When I think of my father and the work that defined him during those years, I recall his checking coats until two-thirty in the morning on weekends, or midnight during the week; and being up at four-thirty in the morning, ready to take the train from Newark to his day job in New York; or to get a head start on the other job seekers.

He worked hard all his life, and he passed that ethic on to me. From my father, I also learned how to get by on very little sleep; to this day, I get up at five-thirty every morning (my father was tougher than I am).

Po Chu-I

The Value of a Simple Life

Po Chu-I lived in the late eighth and early ninth centuries. He is considered one of China's greatest poets. An educator and minor governmental official who rejected pomp and empty ritual, Po Chu-I valued art solely as a means of teaching moral values. He gained popularity as a poet for his simple, direct style. It is said that Po Chu-I was accustomed to reading his poems to an old peasant woman and altering any expressions that she did not comprehend.

At the age of sixty-three, in the year 835, Po Chu-I offered his viewpoint on life-satisfaction in this "Mad Poem Addressed to My Nephews and Nieces":

> The world cheats those who cannot read;
> *I*, happily, have mastered script and pen.
> The world cheats those who hold high office;
> *I* am blessed with high official rank.

The old are often ill;
I, at this day have not an ache or pain.
They are often burdened with ties;
But *I* have finished with marriage and giving in marriage.
No changes happen to disturb the quiet of my mind;
No business comes to impair the vigor of my limbs.
Hence it is that now for ten years
Body and soul have rested in hermit peace.
And all the more, in the last lingering years
What I shall need are very few things.
A single rug to warm me through the winter;
One meal to last me the whole day.
It does not matter that my house is rather small;
One cannot sleep in more than one room!
It does not matter that I have not many horses;
One cannot ride in two coaches at once!
As fortunate as me among the people of the world
Possibly one would find seven out of ten.
As contented as me among a hundred men
Look as you may, you will not find one.
In the affairs of others even fools are wise;
In their own business even sages err.
To no one else would I dare to speak my heart,
So my wild words are addressed to my nephew and nieces.

Henry James

Tips for Effective Writing

Henry James was one of the greatest and most influential novelists in the English language, and certainly preeminent in American literature. Over a fifty-year career, he produced twenty novels including *The Americans, The Europeans, Washington Square,* and *The Portrait of a Lady*.

James never married or had children of his own, but was close to his brother Robertson's oldest son, Edward. In February 1896, Edward was developing his own writing style at Harvard when he received this encouragement from his famous uncle:

> I hope with all my heart that you go through the long period of apprenticeship [as a writer], for the pleasure is worth the pain. You will find out for yourself all sorts of things which will be the steps of your growth, and the joy probably, also, of your soul. . . . Nothing that is worth doing is easy to do.

Live your life as your life comes to you, but, for your work, remember that an art is an art and that you must learn it with every sort of help, with the aid of all the implements.

Read—read—read much. Read everything. You will always observe and live and feel, but for God's sake, be as accomplished as you can.... We live in a frightfully vulgar age, and twaddle and chatter are much imposed upon us. Suspect them—detest them—despise them. Send me all that you do.

C. S. Lewis

———

Clarity and Direction

Acclaimed for his fantasy novels like *The Chronicles of Narnia* and popular religious essays, the Oxford scholar and writer Clive Staples Lewis never had any children of his own, but he was a devoted godfather. And, after becoming famous as a religious writer in the post–World War II era, Lewis maintained an active, fatherly correspondence with youngsters who wrote to him from all over the world.

Realizing that his imaginative tales appealed primarily to children, Lewis felt a sense of responsibility in responding to their questions about life and spirituality. Among his most avid correspondents was a young American girl named Joan, who originally lived in New York City, and then relocated with her family to Florida. Over the years, they exchanged dozens of letters until Lewis's death at the age of sixty-five—but never actually met.

Asked by teen-aged Joan about the secrets of writing effectively, Lewis offered this pungent advice:

1. Always try to use the language so as to make quite clear what you mean and make sure your sentence couldn't mean anything else.

2. Always prefer the plain direct word to the long, vague one. Don't *implement* promises, but *keep* them.

3. Never use abstract nouns when concrete ones will do. If you mean "More people died" don't say "Mortality rose."

4. In writing: Don't use adjectives which merely tell us how you want us to *feel* about the thing you are describing. I mean, instead of telling us a thing was "terrible," describe it so that we'll be terrified. Don't say it was "delightful"; make us say "delightful" when we've read the description. You see, all those words (horrifying, wonderful, hideous, exquisite) are only like saying to your readers "Please will you do the job for me."

5. Don't use words too big for the subject. Don't say "infinitely" when you mean "very"; otherwise you'll have no word left when you want to talk about something *really* infinite.

Jack London

———

Truth

Born in late-nineteenth-century San Francisco, Jack London was one of America's most popular authors. His novels included *The Call of the Wild, White Fang,* and *The Sea Wolf.* He had strong but contradictory attitudes about individual achievement and societal improvement. After his stormy marriage ended, London kept up a relationship—often strained—with his daughter Joan, mainly through correspondence.

Writing from his ranch at Glen Ellen, California, in August and September 1913, the ailing writer sent his twelve-year-old daughter this advice about a key character trait:

> You have your dreams of education. I try to give you the best of my wisdom. . . . Please know that the world belongs to the honest ones, to the true ones, to the right ones, to the ones who talk right out. . . .

INVERSE RATIO.

Small Boy (suddenly). "WHAT ARE HORSES MADE OF, UNCLE?"
Uncle. "OH—FLESH AND BLOOD, OF COURSE."
Small Boy. "I THOUGHT THEY WERE MADE OF CATS'-MEAT."

Remember that truth is the greatest thing in the world. If you will be great, you will be true. If you suppress truth, if you hide truth, if you do not rise up and speak out in meeting . . . [or] without speaking the *whole* truth, then you are less than truth, and by that much are you less than great.

O Joan, it is so remarkably easy just to tell the truth in this world, that I often marvel that there are so many madly foolish, so wretchedly stupid, that they hide truth.

Truth is not merely the best policy. It is the ONLY policy.

J. R. R. Tolkien

―――

Understanding That All Deeds Have a Value

Not for fame or wealth did J.R.R. Tolkien write fantasy epics like *The Hobbit* and *The Lord of the Rings* trilogy. Rather, Tolkien wanted to entertain the four children that he and his wife Mabel were raising in Oxford, where he taught medieval languages. As orphans, both wanted the kind of close, loving family they had never personally known.

Tolkien was able to give his children the gifts of his prodigious imagination by inventing fantasy tales for their amusement. When his son John had trouble falling asleep, Tolkien sat on the corner of his bed and conjured up tales about Carrots, a red-haired boy who climbed into a cuckoo clock and had fantastic adventures. At other times, Tolkien created stories about a villain named Bill Stickers—the name taken from a street sign that read BILL STICKERS WILL BE PROSECUTED—who battled a comic do-gooder named Major Road Ahead. During the 1930s while writing *The Hobbit,* Tolkien avidly solicited the advice of his children about its developing plot and characters.

When Nazi aggression plunged the world into war, Christopher Tolkien joined the Royal Air Force. The frailest of the four children— a heart condition had caused him to be an invalid for several years in his early teens—Christopher had always been close to his father. The two had spent many enjoyable hours together planning *The Lord of the Rings* trilogy. Now, they deepened their relationship by frequent correspondence on such topics as religion, the war, and human suffering. In the spring of 1944, Tolkien offered his worried son this guidance:

> I sometimes feel appalled at the thought of the sum total of human misery all over the world at the present moment: the millions parted, fretting, wasting in unprofitable days—quite apart from torture, pain, death, bereavement, injustice. If anguish were visible, almost the whole of this benighted planet would be enveloped in a dense dark vapor, shrouded from the amazed vision of the heavens! And the products of it all will be mainly evil—historically considered.
>
> But the historical version is, of course, not the only one. All things and deeds have a value in themselves, apart from their "causes" and "effects." No man can estimate what is really happening. . . . All we do know, and that to a large extent by direct experience, is that evil labors with vast power and perpetual

success—in vain: preparing always only the soil for unexpected good to sprout in it. So it is in general and so it is in our lives. . . .

And you were so special a gift to me, in a time of sorrow and mental suffering, and your love, opening at once almost as soon as you were born, foretold to me, as it were in spoken words, that I am consoled every day by the certainty that [it has] no end, and that . . . we have some special bond to last beyond this life. . . . You are inside a very great story!

Bob Dylan

—

What Really Matters

More than just a highly popular songwriter and concert performer, in his youth Bob Dylan became a symbol for his entire generation. In the tumultuous years of the 1960s, his impassioned songs like "Blowin' in the Wind" and "The Times, They Are A-Changin'" were indelibly associated with social causes like civil rights, anti-war rallies, and candlelit marches. They gained him the stature of a cultural icon.

Besides his prodigious accomplishments as a songwriter and performer, Dylan is also the father of five children. He married young and first experienced fatherhood at the age of twenty-five.

In early 1972, Dylan was thirty years old, and perhaps first sensing the passage of time in his own life, when he composed a song for his infant son, Jacob. Entitled "Forever Young," its tender sentiments, tuneful melody, and poetic imagery make it one of Dylan's most beloved songs today:

May God bless and keep you always. May your wishes all come
   true.
May you always do for others, and let others do for you.
May you build a ladder to the stars and climb on every rung.
And, may you stay forever young.
May you grow up to be righteous. May you grow up to be true.
May you always know the truth and see the light surrounding
   you.
May you always be courageous, stand upright and be strong.
And, may you stay forever young.
Forever young. Forever young. May you stay forever young.
May your hands always be busy. May your feet always be swift.
May you have a strong foundation when the winds of changes
   shift.
May your heart always be joyful. May your song always be sung.
And, may you stay forever young.
Forever young. Forever young. May you stay forever young.

F. Scott Fitzgerald

━━━

To Worry and Not to Worry

F. Scott Fitzgerald's wife, Zelda, suffered for years from suicidal depression that resulted in frequent stays in the hospital. Consequently Fitzgerald did most of the parenting for their only child, Frances Scott ("Scottie.") The author of *The Jazz Age, The Great Gatsby,* and other novels, short stories, and screenplays was a devoted father. He taught Scottie riddles and limericks, played Hangman with her, and encouraged her to read his favorite children's books, Thackeray's *The Rose and the Ring* and Kipling's *Just-So-Stories*. He did not want Scottie to become bookish, however, and often played tennis and croquet with her, and also taught her boxing.

In the summer of 1933, eleven-year-old Scottie was away at camp when she received this pithy, fatherly wisdom. Its humorous, yet provocative advice remains relevant for many adolescents today:

Things to worry about:
Worry about courage
worry about cleanliness

Worry about efficiency
Worry about horsemanship . . .

Things not to worry about:
    Don't worry about popular opinion
    Don't worry about dolls
    Don't worry about the past
    Don't worry about the future
    Don't worry about growing up
    Don't worry about anybody getting ahead of you
    Don't worry about triumph
    Don't worry about failure unless it comes through your
        own fault
    Don't worry about mosquitoes
    Don't worry about flies
    Don't worry about insects in general
    Don't worry about parents
    Don't worry about boys
    Don't worry about disappointments
    Don't worry about pleasures
    Don't worry about satisfactions

Things to think about:
    What am I really aiming at?

William Hazlitt

━━━

Conduct in the World

William Hazlitt was a leading essayist and critic in early nineteenth-century England. He wrote with enthusiasm and sensitivity about literature, including Shakespearean drama and contemporary poetry. In his collection of personal essays entitled *Table Talk,* published in 1822, Hazlitt intriguingly described his early encounters with the poets Samuel Coleridge and William Wordsworth.

Hazlitt's only child was William Jr. According to family friends, the lad was often spoiled lavishly by his devoted father. In early 1822, Hazlitt sent this guidance about life to his eleven-year-old son:

> My dear little fellow, you are now going to settle at school, and may consider this as your first entrance into the world. As my health is so indifferent, and I may not be with you long, I wish to leave you with some advice (the best I can) for your conduct in life, both that it may be of use to you, and as something to

remember me by. I may be at least able to caution you against my own errors, if nothing else.

It is a good old rule to hope for the best. Always believe things to be right, till you find them the contrary; and even then, instead of irritating yourself against them, endeavor to put up with them as well as you can, if you cannot alter them.

Learn never to conceive a prejudice against others because you know nothing of them. It is bad reasoning and makes enemies of half the world. Do not think ill of them, till they behave ill toward you; and then strive to avoid the faults you see in them. This will disarm their hostility sooner than pique or resentment or complaint. Never despise anyone for anything he cannot help—least of all, his poverty.

You cannot always be with me, and perhaps it is as well that you cannot. But you must not expect others to show the same concern about you as I should. The first lesson to learn is that there are other people in the world besides yourself. . . . The more airs of childish self-importance you give yourself, you will only expose yourself to be the more thwarted and laughed at. You were not born a king's son to destroy or dictate to others; you can only expect to share their fate, or settle your differences amicably with them.

Do not begin to quarrel with the world too soon: for, bad as it may be, it is the best we have to live in—here. If railing would have made it better, it would have been reformed long ago; but as this is not to be hoped for at present, the best way is to slide through it as contentedly and innocently as we may.

We may laugh or weep at the madness of mankind; we have no right to vilify them, for our own sakes or theirs.

References

Alsop, Joseph W. *I've Seen the Best of It*. New York: Norton, 1992.

Aristide, Jean-Bertrand. *Aristide: An Autobiography*. Translated by Linda M. Maloney. Maryknoll, New York: Orbis, 1993.

Asimov, Isaac. *I. Asimov, A Memoir*. Garden City: Doubleday, 1994.

Bade, William Frederic. *The Life and Letters of John Muir, Volume II*. Boston: Houghton Mifflin, 1924.

Baldwin, Neil. *Edison: Inventing the Century*. New York: Hyperion, 1995.

Beatty, Jack. *The Rascal King: The Life and Times of James Michael Curley, 1874–1958*. Reading, Mass.: Addison-Wesley, 1992.

Bedell, Madelon. *The Alcotts: Biography of a Family*. New York: Clarkson Potter, 1980.

Benny, Jack and Joan Benny. *Sunday Nights at Seven: The Jack Benny Story*. New York: Warner, 1990.

Berg, A. Scott. *Goldwyn: A Biography*. New York: Knopf, 1989.

Brockway, Wallace and Bart Keith Winer, Eds. *A Second Treasury of the World's Great Letters*. New York: Simon & Schuster, 1941.

Brown, Judith M. *Gandhi: Prisoner of Hope*. New Haven: Yale University Press, 1989.

Browning, Robert. *Letters of Robert Browning*. Collected by Thomas J. Wise. Edited with an introduction and notes by Thurman L. Hood. New Haven: Yale University Press, 1933.

Bruce, Robert V. *Bell: Alexander Graham Bell and the Conquest of Solitude*. Boston: Little, Brown, 1973.

Burch, Cyril and Donald Keene, Eds. *Anthology of Chinese Literature from Early Times to the Fourteenth Century*. New York: Grove Weidenfeld, 1965.

Bucky, Peter A. *The Private Albert Einstein*. Kansas City: Andrews and McMeel, 1993.

Burton, Humphrey. *Leonard Bernstein*. Garden City, N.Y.: Doubleday, 1994.

Buscaglia, Leo, *Papa, My Father*. New York: Morrow, 1989.

Carroll, Lewis. *The Letters of Lewis Carroll, Volume Two: 1886–1898*. Edited by Morton N. Cohen and Roger Lancelyn Green. New York: Oxford University Press, 1979.

Carter, James Earl and Rosalynne Carter. *Everything to Gain: Making the Most of the Rest of Your Life*. New York: Bantam, 1987.

Cohen, Hennig and Donald Yanella. *Herman Melville's Malcolm Letter: "Man's Final Lore."* New York: Fordham University Press, 1992.

Coleridge, Samuel Taylor. *Collected Letters of Samuel Taylor Coleridge, Volume III: 1807–1814*. Edited by Earl Leslie Griggs. Oxford: Clarendon Press, 1959.

Collier, James Lincoln. *Benny Goodman and the Swing Era*. New York: Oxford University Press, 1989.

Cuomo, Mario. *Diaries of Mario M. Cuomo: The Campaign for Governor*. New York: Random House, 1984.

Dallek, Robert. *Lone Star Rising, Lyndon Johnson and His Times, 1908–1960*. New York: Oxford University Press, 1991.

Dickens, Charles. *Selected Letters of Charles Dickens*. Edited and arranged by David Paroissien. Boston: Twayne, 1985.

Dylan, Bob. "Forever Young" from *Bob Dylan at Budokan*. Columbia Records, 1979.

Emerson, Ralph Waldo, *The Letters of Ralph Waldo Emerson*, volume six. Edited by Ralph L. Rusk. New York: Columbia University Press, 1939.

Ernst, Joseph W., Ed. *Dear Father/Dear Son: Correspondence of John D. Rockefeller and John D. Rockefeller, Jr.* New York: Fordham University Press, 1994.

Estrada, Francisco Lopez, Ed. *Antología de Epistoles. Cartas Selectas de los Mas Famosos Autores de la Historía Universal.* Barcelona: Editorial Labor, 1961.

Faulkner, William. *Selected Letters of William Faulkner.* Edited by Joseph Blotner. New York: Random House, 1977.

Frost, Robert and Elinor Frost. *Family Letters of Robert and Elinor Frost.* Edited by Arnold Grade. Albany: State University of New York Press, 1972.

Fields, W. C. *By Himself: His Intended Autobiography.* Commentary by Ronald J. Fields, Englewood Cliffs, N.J.: Prentice-Hall, 1973.

Fitzgerald, F. Scott. *A Life in Letters.* Edited by Matthew J. Bruccoli and Judith S. Baughman. New York: Scribner's, 1994.

Flaubert, Gustave. *Letters.* Selected with an introduction by Richard Rumbold. Translated by J. M. Cohen. London: Weidenfeld & Nicolson, 1950.

Freud, Sigmund. *Letters of Sigmund Freud.* Selected and edited by Ernest L. Freud. Translated by Tania and James Stern. New York: Basic Books, 1961.

Gill, Brendan. *Many Masks: A Life of Frank Lloyd Wright.* New York: Putnam's, 1987.

Harnsbinger, Caroline. *Mark Twain, Family Man.* New York: Citadel Press, 1960.

Harte, Bret. *The Letters of Bret Harte.* Assembled and edited by Geoffrey Bret Harte. London: Hodder and Stoughton, 1926.

Harris, Julia Collier. *The Life and Letters of Joel Chandler Harris.* Boston: Houghton Mifflin, 1918.

Hazlitt, William. *The Letters of William Hazlitt.* Edited by Herschel Moreland Sikes, Willard Hallam Bonner, and Gerald Lahey. New York: Oxford University Press, 1978.

Hearst, William Randolph Jr. *The Hearsts, Father and Son.* New York: Roberts Rinehart, 1991.

Hemingway, George M. *Papa: A Personal Memoir*. Boston: Houghton Mifflin, 1976.

Heylin, Clinton. *Bob Dylan: Behind the Shades*. New York: Summit, 1991.

Hill, Hamlin. *Mark Twain: God's Fool*. New York: Harper & Row, 1973.

Hoffman, Edward. *The Drive for Self: Alfred Adler and the Founding of Individual Psychology*. Reading, Mass.: Addison-Wesley, 1994.

Horowitz, David, Ed. *Shalom, Friend: The Life and Legacy of Yitzhak Rabin*. New York: Newmarket Press, 1996.

Howells, William Dean. *Life in Letters of William Dean Howells*, Volume Two. Edited by Mildred Howells. Garden City, N.Y.: Doubleday, Doran & Company, 1928.

Huxley, Aldous. *Letters of Aldous Huxley*. Edited by Grover Smith. London: Chatto & Windus, 1969.

Irving, Washington. *Letters, volume II, 1823–1838*. Edited by Ralph M. Aderman, Herbert L. Kleinfeld, and Jennifer S. Banks. Boston: Twayne, 1979.

James, Henry. *Letters, volume IV, 1895–1916*. Edited by Leon Edel. Cambridge: Harvard University Press, 1984.

James, William. *The Selected Letters of William James*. Edited with an introduction by Elizabeth Hardwick. New York: Farrar, Straus & Giroux, 1961.

Jefferson, Thomas. *The Family Letters of Thomas Jefferson*. Edited by Edwin Morris Britts and James Adam Bear Jr. Columbia: University of Missouri Press, 1966.

Kobler, Franz, Ed. *Letters of Jews Throughout the Ages*. New York: East and West Library, 1978.

Koch, Edward I. *Citizen Koch: An Autobiography*. New York: St. Martin, 1992.

Lake, Stuart N. *Wyatt Earp, Frontier Marshall*. New York: Pocket Books, 1994.

London, Jack. *Letters From Jack London*. Edited by King Hendricks and Irving Shepard. New York: Odyssey, 1965.

Lowell, James Russell. *Letters of James Russell Lowell*. Edited by Chales Eliot Norton. New York: Harper & Brothers, 1894.

Lewis, Clive S. *Letters to Children*. Edited by Lyle W. Dorsett and Marjorie Lamp Mead. New York: Macmillan, 1985.

Longfellow, Henry Wadsworth. *The Letters of Henry Wadsworth Longfellow, Volume 5: 1866–1874*. Edited by Andrew Hilen, Cambridge: Harvard University Press, 1982.

Lopate, Phillip, Ed. *The Art of the Personal Essay: An Anthology from the Classical Era to the Present*. New York: Anchor, 1994.

Lowenstein, Roger. *Buffett: The Making of an American Capitalist*. New York: Random House, 1995.

MacArthur, Douglas. *Reminiscences*. New York: McGraw-Hill, 1964.

Manchester, William. *American Caesar: Douglas MacArthur, 1880–1964*. Boston: Little, Brown, 1978.

Martin, Ralph G. *A Hero for Our Time: An Intimate Story of the Kennedy Years*. New York: Macmillan, 1983.

Marx, Arthur. *My Life with Groucho: A Son's Eye View*. London: Robson Books, 1988.

Melville, Herman. *The Letters of Herman Melville*. Edited by Merrell R. Davis and William H. Gilman. New Haven: Yale University Press, 1960.

Monegal, Emir Rodriguez. *Jorge Luis Borges: A Literary Biography*. New York: E.P. Dutton, 1978.

Moore, Ruth. *Niels Bohr: The Man, His Science and The World They Changed*. New York: Knopf, 1966.

Nixon, Richard. *The Memoirs of Richard Nixon*. New York: Grosset & Dunlap, 1978.

Oates, Stephen B. *Let the Trumpet Sound: The Life of Martin Luther King Jr*. New York: Harper & Row, 1982.

———. *William Faulkner: The Man and the Artist, a Biography*. New York: Harper & Row, 1987.

O'Brien, Michael. *Vince: A Personal Biography of Vince Lombardi*. New York: Morrow, 1987.

Pollock, Dale. *Skywalking: The Life and Films of George Lucas*. New York: Harmony Books, 1983.

Powell, Colin L. *My American Journey*. New York: Random House, 1995.

Raleigh, Walter. *The Letters of Sir Walter Raleigh (1879–1922)*, Volume II. Edited by Lady Raleigh. New York: Macmillan, 1926.

Reston, James. *Deadline: A Memoir*. New York: Random House, 1991.

Riemer, Jack and Nathaniel Stampfer. *So That Your Values Live On: Ethical Wills and How to Prepare Them*. Woodstock, Vermont: Jewish Lights, 1991.

Robinson, David. *Chaplin, His Life and Art*. New York: McGraw-Hill, 1985.

Roosevelt, Theodore. *Theodore Roosevelt's Letters to His Children*. Edited by Joseph Bucklin Bishop. New York: Scribner's, 1919.

Sanders, Thomas E. and Walter W. Peek. *Literature of the American Indian*. New York: Glencoe, 1973.

Schuster, Lincoln M., Ed. *A Treasury of the World's Great Letters*. New York: Simon & Schuster, 1940.

Solomon, Maynard. *Mozart*. New York: HarperCollins, 1995.

Symonds, John Addington. *The Letters of John Addington Symonds, Volume III: 1885–1893*. Edited by Herbert M. Schueller and Robert L. Parker. Detroit: Wayne State University Press, 1969.

The Noble Qur'an. Translated by Muhammad Taqui-ud-Din Al-Hilali and Muhammad Muhsin Khan. Riyadh, Saudi Arabia: Dar-es-Salaam, 1994.

The Oxford Annotated Bible. Edited by Herbert G. May and Bruce M. Metzger. New York: Oxford University Press, 1962.

Tolkien, J.R.R. *The Letters of J.R.R. Tolkien*. Selected and edited by Humphrey Carpenter. Boston: Houghton Mifflin, 1981.

Thomas, Bob. *Walt Disney: An American Original*. New York: Simon & Schuster, 1976.

Tolstoy, Leo. *Tolstoy's Letters, Volume II: 1880–1910*. Selected, edited, and translated by R. F. Christian. London: Athlone Press, 1978.

Trillin, Calvin. *Messagtes from my Father*. New York: Farrar, Straus & Giroux, 1996.

Truman, Margaret. *Letters from Father*. New York: Arbor House, 1981.

Valentine, Alan, Ed. *Fathers to Sons, Advice Without Consent*. Norman: University of Oklahoma Press, 1963.

Waley, Arthur. *More Translations from the Chinese*. New York: Knopf, 1937.

Warren, Robert Penn. *Portrait of a Father*. Lexington: University of Kentucky Press, 1988.

Watson, Thomas J., Jr. *Father, Son & Co.: My Life at IBM and Beyond*. New York: Bantam, 1990.

Waugh, Evelyn. *The Letters of Evelyn Waugh*. Edited by Mark Amory. New Haven: Ticknor & Fields, 1980.

Williams, William Carlos. *The Selected Letters of William Carlos Williams*. Edited with an introduction by John C. Thirwall. New York: McDowell, Osolensky, 1957.

Wright, John Lloyd. *My Father Who Is on Earth*. New York: Putnam's, 1962.

Yeats, J. B. *Letters to his Son W. B. Yeats and Others*. Edited with a memoir by Joseph Stone. New York: Dutton, 1946.

Zamir, Israel. *Journey to My Father, Isaac Bashevis Singer*. Translated by Barbara Harshaw. New York: Arcade, 1995.